# EQUALITY

## *in*

# CHRIST?

---

*Galatians 3:28*
*and the Gender Dispute*

---

## RICHARD W. HOVE

CROSSWAY BOOKS • WHEATON, ILLINOIS
A DIVISION OF GOOD NEWS PUBLISHERS

Cover design: David LaPlaca

First printing, 1999

Printed in the United States of America

**Library of Congress Cataloging-in-Publication Data**

Hove, Richard W., 1957–
    Equality in Christ? : Galatians 3:28 and the gender dispute / Richard W. Hove.
       p.   cm.
    Includes bibliographical references and index.
    ISBN 1-58134-103-2 (alk. paper)
    1. Bible. N.T. Galatians III, 28—Criticism, interpretation, etc.
    2. Sex role—Bible teaching. I. Title.
BS2685.6.S37H68  1999
227'.406—dc21
                                 99-23342
                                    CIP

| 15 | 14 | 13 | 12 | 11 | 10 | 09 | 08 | 07 | 06 | 05 | 04 | 03 | 02 | 01 | 00 | 99 |
|----|----|----|----|----|----|----|----|----|----|----|----|----|----|----|----|----|
| 15 | 14 | 13 | 12 | 11 | 10 | 9 | 8 | 7 | 6 | 5 | 4 | 3 | 2 | 1 | | |

*"There is neither Jew nor Greek, slave nor free, male nor female, for you are all one in Christ Jesus."*

—Galatians 3:28

*To Sonya.*

*She is a gift of inestimable value,*
*and I thank God it is my lot to share life with her.*
*She is worthy of far greater tribute than*
*this meager dedication page.*

# CONTENTS

# PREFACE

Before there was a thought of crafting this material into a book, it lay in academic obscurity, known only to a few as a master's thesis. It might have stayed in that state forever except for the encouragement of three friends—Dr. D. A. Carson, Dr. Grant Osborne, and Dr. Wayne Grudem. They suggested I have it published and introduced me to Dr. Lane Dennis at Crossway Books. Crossway Books asked if they could give it a second life as a book. You now hold the end result.

I've made some changes to the original thesis to make it more suitable as a book, though the vast majority of the original work remains intact. The Greek text, for the most part, has been relegated to the footnotes in order to make the study more accessible to readers lacking a knowledge of Greek. If you do know Greek it is all there for you. If you don't, everything is translated and you should have no difficulty following the arguments.

I trust that this study is stronger for having first been a thesis. Academic theses are generally able to focus intensely on a single topic or passage, delving into issues that perhaps have not been explored in the past. Good theses are able to present an extended argument in a systematic fashion that thoroughly deals with all the issues and interacts with most, if not all, the secondary literature. Theses are written with the knowledge that they must be defended publicly before an academic audience. And, in this case, a thesis provides a wonderful opportunity to devote a large amount of time to research and study. As part of my master's program I was able to do virtually nothing but research and think about Galatians 3:28 for nine months.

If this study had been first created as a book I would have probably done a few things differently. I might, for example, have limited the number of footnotes or provided more colorful transitions or illustrations. Who knows, I might even have been able to add a picture or two (my children think all books should have pictures!). But then again, if this had begun as a book perhaps it would lack some of the strengths of a thesis. In the end, I hope this work has built upon all its strengths as a thesis and has added what is necessary to be a good academic book.

# ACKNOWLEDGMENTS

I am deeply indebted to many who have made unique contributions to this study on Galatians 3:28. Dr. Wayne Grudem first prompted my interest in the crucial issue of manhood and womanhood many years ago. His friendship, mentoring, and interest in my work are a great encouragement.

Dr. D. A. Carson patiently guided my thesis research, pointing out my errors and answering many questions on diverse subjects. Being mentored by him was an experience for which I will always be grateful. I learned from him, among other things, that most arguments contain a morsel of truth; the challenge is to avoid the lure of reductionistic thinking and allow all the evidence its due. Nearly any position can be made to look appealing based on a portion of the evidence. Dr. Carson's breadth of knowledge enlightened and challenged me; his pastoral spirit and friendship encouraged me. This study would doubtless have been substantially different, and weaker, without his help, and it is with much gratitude that I acknowledge the unique importance of his contribution.

Many outside the academic community have assisted in the production of this book. Many families and churches have financially supported our ministry with Campus Crusade for Christ for the past twenty years; this book would never have been possible without their loyal commitment to our family and ministry. Many friends—in our small group, in our church, and within the Trinity Seminary community—have enriched our lives during our Trinity years. Quite a few of these friends heard more about Galatians 3:28 than they ever wanted to know. Special thanks to Margaret (you don't care much about the details of Galatians 3:28, but you sure care for Sonya and me); Howard and

Nancy (you've sweetened our lives in so many ways); Ed and Deb and Tom and Gayle (you've been friends through it all); Dennis and Lavon (your friendship and encouragement are such a blessing to us); and Larry and Norma (thanks for believing in what we do).

My children—Andrew, Meagan, and Mark—have made their own little sacrifices to help this work along. Often they have wondered when Daddy would get off the computer. Usually this is because they want to play with me, but increasingly it is because they want to take over my computer. They are such a joy, and I love them dearly. Now we can take more bike rides, wrestle more, and have more tea parties.

Nobody has supported and encouraged me during the writing of this book more than my bride, Sonya. She is of inestimable value, believing in me, cheering me on, nourishing my soul, taking care of our clan, adding wise counsel, and personally bringing daily joy to my task-filled world. Where would I be without you?

Lastly, any acknowledgment page would be seriously deficient without a tribute to our great God, who has made all this possible. To him be all the glory.

# List of Abbreviations

**BAGD** *Greek-English Lexicon of the New Testament and Early Christian Literature* (Bauer, Arndt, Gingrich, and Danker)

**BDF** *Greek Grammar of the New Testament and Other Early Christian Literature* (Blass, Debrunner, and Funk)

**EDNT** *Exegetical Dictionary of the New Testament* (eds. Balz and Schneider)

**JETS** *Journal of the Evangelical Theological Society*

**JSNT Sup** *Journal for the Study of the New Testament*—Supplement Series

**LSJ** *Greek-English Lexicon* (Liddell, Scott, Jones)

**MM** *Vocabulary of the Greek Testament* (Moulton and Milligan)

**NA 27** Nestle/Aland Greek New Testament, 27th ed.

**TDNT** *Theological Dictionary of the New Testament*

**TLG** Thesaurus Linguae Graecae Computer Data Base

**UBS 3** United Bible Society Greek New Testament, 3rd ed.

# Introduction:
# The Battle over Galatians 3:28

Over the past twenty to thirty years a great debate has raged regarding the roles of men and women. Should women, for example, be allowed to fight in combat situations? Historically the answer to this question has been no, but today this question is often answered in the affirmative; military combat is an option for both men and women. Can women compete in the traditionally male sports, such as football or wrestling? The consensus is changing; many now insist that to exclude women who desire to participate in these sports is to deny them equal opportunity.

Closely related to questions about sexual roles are questions regarding equality: Have women been given the same opportunities as men? Have they been afforded similar credit for their accomplishments? Have businesses, for example, traditionally the domain of men, unfairly excluded women from top management positions? Have women pilots in the military received the same treatment as men? Have women been discriminated against by not receiving the same scholarship funding as men in college sports? Is it inequitable to have male-only military academies? These specific controversies simply serve to illustrate that it is hardly possible to overemphasize the importance and intensity of the present struggle concerning issues related to manhood and womanhood.

The church has not been a passive observer of this struggle. It has found itself embroiled in controversies not unlike those in the rest of society: Are men and women "equal" in God's sight? Have women been discriminated against in the church, of all places? Does God's Word teach that there are unique roles for a husband and a wife in marriage?

Are there unique roles for men and women in the church? Is Promise Keepers a wonderful organization helping husbands love and lead their wives and families, or is it an organization perpetuating a dangerously distorted hierarchical view of marriage? Are present translations of the Bible unwittingly sexist? Bible-believing evangelicals have struggled with questions related to manhood and womanhood as intensely as the rest of society.

A thorough evaluation of the causes of this sexual "crisis" is not possible here; it is sufficient to note that the battle is important for all parties involved. Only the naive can witness the ongoing struggle over men's and women's roles and label it a "secondary issue." On the contrary, the struggle over sexual identity and roles is critical because sexuality is a crucial part of what it means to be human. God created sexual beings, and if he created them with unique differences and roles, these are not ancillary addenda to humanness, but rather are part of the core of what it means to be human. In fact, the emotional intensity that characterizes this struggle is evidence itself that this is not a secondary issue. The reason this debate is so heated—there are, it seems, no neutral parties—is because each person deeply cares about his or her sexual identity. This identity is, for each individual, monumentally important to how one views one's self and life. The debate is important, and it is not going away.

## THE IMPORTANCE OF GALATIANS 3:28

In Galatians 3:28 Paul writes, "There is neither Jew nor Greek, slave nor free, male nor female, for you are all one in Christ Jesus."[1] This passage has become a critical text in the contemporary debate over the roles of men and women in the church, in the home, and in society. For example, the web page of Christians for Biblical Equality states, "Christians for Biblical Equality is an organization of Christians who believe the Bible, properly interpreted, teaches the fundamental equality of men and women of all racial and ethnic groups, all economic classes, and all age groups, based on biblical teachings summarized in Galatians 3:28."[2] Rebecca Groothuis, in her recent book *Good News for Women: A*

---

[1] All Scripture references in this study are from the NIV unless otherwise noted.
[2] www.cbeinternational.org.

*Biblical Picture of Gender Equality,* writes, "Of all the texts that support biblical equality, Galatians 3:26-28 is probably the most important."[3] In her estimation this verse is the ultimate biblical statement concerning gender equality. When David Scholer was recently installed as professor of New Testament at Fuller Theological Seminary, he chose to address the issue of the ministry of women in the church. Four main evidences have emerged, he argued, for the "full participation of women in the ministry of the church."[4] First, women were the first eyewitnesses and proclaimers of the resurrection. Second, women, just like men, received the full power of the Holy Spirit. Third, the Bible portrays many women who actually exercised authority and leadership among the people of God. Fourth, Paul declares that "there is no longer . . . male and female; for all of you are one in Christ Jesus."[5] In Scholer's opinion, Galatians 3:28 is *"the fundamental Pauline theological basis for the inclusion of women and men as equal and mutual partners in all of the ministries of the church."*[6] These examples simply illustrate that, for some, Galatians 3:28 is more than a key text in the debate over men's and women's roles in the home and church; rather, it is the *fundamental* or *most important* statement in the New Testament on this issue.[7]

There are, of course, those who disagree with this assessment of Galatians 3:28. They believe Galatians 3:28 says little about gender-based roles in the church. Ronald Fung comments, "Paul's statement is *not* concerned with the role relationships of men and women within the Body of Christ but rather with their common initiation/integration into it through faith and baptism."[8] In an early work on this subject, James Hurley writes,

---

[3] Rebecca Merrill Groothuis, *Good News for Women: A Biblical Picture of Gender Equality* (Grand Rapids, Mich.: Baker, 1997), 25.
[4] David M. Scholer, "Galatians 3:28 and the Ministry of Women in the Church," in *Theology, News and Notes* (Pasadena, Calif.: Fuller Theological Seminary, June 1998), 19-22.
[5] Ibid., 19.
[6] Ibid., 20, italics his.
[7] J. W. Cooper, in his *A Cause for Division? Women in Office and the Unity of the Church,* establishes "the analogy of Scripture" along a continuum stretching from "The First Word" of Genesis 1:26-28 to "The Last Word" of Revelation 22:5, with "Paul's Middle Word" being Galatians 3:28. This is indeed a high estimation of the importance of Galatians 3:28! Cited by Robert W. Yarbrough, "The Hermeneutics of 1 Timothy 2:9-15," in *Women in the Church: A Fresh Analysis of 1 Timothy 2:9-15,* eds. Andreas J. Köstenberger, Thomas R. Schreiner, and H. Scott Baldwin (Grand Rapids, Mich.: Baker, 1995), 191, n. 167.
[8] Ronald Y. K. Fung, "Ministry in the New Testament," in *The Church and the Bible and the World,* ed. D. A. Carson (Grand Rapids, Mich.: Baker, 1987), 183-184, italics mine.

Our study of the context of Galatians 3:28 has shown that Paul was not reflecting upon relations *within* the body of Christ when he had the text penned. He was thinking about the basis of membership in the body of Christ. This means that it is an error to say that "all one" in Christ means that there are no distinctions within the body.[9]

S. Lewis Johnson agrees:

There is no reason to claim that Galatians 3:28 supports an egalitarianism of function in the church. It does plainly teach an egalitarianism of privilege in the covenantal union of believers in Christ.[10]

John Piper and Wayne Grudem comment,

The context of Galatians 3:28 makes abundantly clear the sense in which men and women are equal in Christ: they are equally justified by faith (v. 24), equally free from the bondage of legalism (v. 25), equally children of God (v. 26), equally clothed with Christ (v. 27), equally possessed by Christ (v. 29), and equally heirs of the promises to Abraham (v. 29). . . . Galatians 3:28 does not abolish gender-based roles established by God and redeemed by Christ.[11]

As the controversy over the roles of men and women has intensified, evangelical scholars have appropriately given increased attention to Galatians 3:28. It is safe to say that Galatians 3:28 is one of the most debated, and important, verses in the dispute over the biblical teaching on the roles of men and women.

## THE CONTRIBUTION OF THIS STUDY

The purpose of this study is to examine the lexical, syntactical, and contextual issues that are important for an accurate interpretation of Galatians 3:28. Though many articles and books have addressed the implications of Galatians 3:28, very few of these have given sufficient

---

[9] James B. Hurley, *Man and Woman in Biblical Perspective* (Grand Rapids, Mich.: Zondervan, 1981), 127, italics his.
[10] S. Lewis Johnson, "Role Distinctions in the Church," in *Recovering Biblical Manhood and Womanhood*, eds. John Piper and Wayne Grudem (Wheaton, Ill.: Crossway, 1991), 164.
[11] John Piper and Wayne Grudem, "An Overview of Central Concerns: Questions and Answers," in ibid., 71-72.

attention to the exegetical details of the passage. This study will attempt to address these exegetical issues.

This book consists of four distinct sections, corresponding to the four chapter divisions:

Chapter 1 examines the flow of Paul's argument in Galatians 3–4. Galatians 3:28 is a piece of a larger whole, and it is necessary to understand the broader context in order to interpret the individual verse. Many erroneous interpretations of Galatians 3:28 have been spawned because the context of the passage was neglected.

Chapter 2 addresses the exegetical issues in Galatians 3:26-29, with special attention to lexical and syntactical issues. Many issues, such as the meaning of the phrase "for you are all one in Christ Jesus," have not been given the attention they deserve.

Chapter 3 marshals the evidence found in the previous two sections and presents and defends an interpretation of Galatians 3:28.

Chapter 4 interacts with a recent egalitarian interpretation of Galatians 3:28.

As it is impossible to do everything in a single study, this study will not deal with several interesting and important questions. Though it is certainly important, for example, to integrate all of the biblical texts on the roles of men and women into a coherent whole, that is not the purpose of this study.[12]

Similarly, it is not the purpose of this work to answer the plethora of questions related to manhood and womanhood. Paul and other divinely inspired authors provide far more information about manhood and womanhood than what is found in Galatians 3:28. One should not expect Galatians 3:28, or this study, to provide an answer for every question about manhood and womanhood. The challenge of this work is to allow Galatians 3:28 to speak for itself without reading into it from other passages. There are legitimate hermeneutical questions related to the issue of biblical manhood and womanhood, but most of these arise when one tries to synthesize all of the New Testament teaching on the subject. For example, some have argued that Galatians 3:28 should be

---

[12] For a bibliography of evangelical books on this topic see *CBMW News,* vol. 1, no. 2 (November 1995): 12. This reference only cites *books* from evangelical authors. In addition, there are many, many journal articles that address this topic that are not included in that list.

a "'window' text through which to adjudicate other Pauline texts,"[13] and that texts such as 1 Timothy 2 should be seen and interpreted in light of Galatians 3:28. But because the focus of this work is Galatians 3:28, and not a comprehensive theology of biblical manhood and womanhood, we will not delve into hermeneutical questions unless they directly affect the meaning and significance of Galatians 3:28. I will suggest that it is possible to determine the meaning and significance of Galatians 3:28 without encountering difficult hermeneutical obstacles.

The importance of Galatians 3:28 in the contemporary dispute over gender roles is such that it is worthy of a study devoted solely to its meaning and significance. That is the goal of this work: to produce a thorough exegetical study of Galatians 3:28 that will help clarify the meaning and significance of this one verse. I hope that, by thoroughly dealing with this one critical text, progress will be made toward resolving the larger question of a biblical theology of manhood and womanhood.

I trust, however, that this book will accomplish something more than a good exegetical study of Galatians 3:28. I trust that our search for *clarity* on the meaning and significance of this verse will be conducted in a *charitable* manner. My hope for charity is as strong as my desire for clarity. I have seen friendships and churches torn apart by this issue; people have even lost jobs and reputations for speaking out on this topic. Because of the highly emotional nature of the current gender dispute, it is easy to demean those who disagree with your position. I trust that I have dealt kindly with all those whose works I interact with in these pages, especially those with whom I most disagree. In many cases opposing sides on this issue have unfairly distorted the other's position.[14] At best this does nothing to further the discussion. At worst, brothers

---

[13] Scholer, "Galatians 3:28," 20.

[14] Examples can be found on both sides of this issue. Patricia Gundry, in the opening essay in *Women, Authority, and the Bible*, writes, "There is but one central and watershed question in this conflicted issue: Are women fully human? All other questions and issues are peripheral to this question." Patricia Gundry, "Why We're Here," in *Women, Authority, and the Bible*, ed. Alvera Mickelsen (Downers Grove, Ill.: InterVarsity, 1986), 20. The implication is that those who disagree with her believe that women are not fully human. I don't know of any credible spokesperson in this dispute who believes that women are not fully human; to define the dispute in these terms is unnecessarily inflammatory.

David Ayers, writing in *Recovering Biblical Manhood and Womanhood*, states, "[Christian feminists] . . . have the same tendencies toward education and 'reform,' the same suspicion of full-time motherhood, the same support for abortion, the same sexual 'tolerance,' etc., as the secularists." David

and sisters who share in one Christ are angered by false characterizations and misrepresentations, often resulting in greater disunity. There is nothing fair or noble in misrepresenting someone else's position for one's own benefit, and hopefully this work has fairly represented all whom it has cited. If I have failed in this goal, I sincerely desire to be informed.

I have also made every effort to cite credible spokespersons on both sides of this issue. One could cite extreme scholars on each side, but this again fails to profit anyone. I trust that every reader will feel that his or her position has been put forward in its best light, even if he or she disagrees with my conclusions. If my attempt to deal kindly and fairly with all has fallen short, it is assuredly not because of lack of good intent.

---

J. Ayers, "The Inevitability of Failure: The Assumptions and Implementations of Modern Feminism," in *Recovering Biblical Manhood and Womanhood,* eds. John Piper and Wayne Grudem (Wheaton, Ill.: Crossway, 1991), 321. Ayers's characterization of evangelical feminists strikes me as both unfair and untrue. Granted, *some* "evangelical" feminists might fit his description, but as a whole most who would invoke the label "evangelical" would take a stand against abortion and sexual "tolerance."

# THE BROAD CONTEXT:
# GALATIANS 3-4

Any endeavor to understand Galatians 3:28 must consider the purpose and function of the verse within the broader argument of Galatians 3–4. Paul did not begin his discussion with 3:28, nor did he pen this verse as a solitary proverbial saying. Rather, the meaning of "there is neither Jew nor Greek, slave nor free, male nor female, for you are all one in Christ Jesus" is largely determined by its context. Thus, prior to exegeting Galatians 3:28 (in chapter 2), and discussing its meaning and significance (in chapter 3), this chapter will investigate the broader emphases, issues, and arguments of Galatians 3–4 that are most pertinent to the interpretation of Galatians 3:28. At the onset we will need to examine briefly two preliminary issues that are significant for the interpretation of the book of Galatians: i) who are Paul's opponents in Galatia? and ii) what is the problem in the church in Galatia?

## THE GALATIAN SITUATION

Paul wrote Galatians in response to false teaching (a "different gospel," 1:6) propagated by a group of "agitators" (5:12) who desired "to make a good impression outwardly" (6:12). These opponents and their theology precipitated Paul's letter. Knowing the identity and beliefs of this group would greatly facilitate a proper understanding of Paul's response to them, but as with most ancient literature, it is not easy to reconstruct the precise situation that confronted Paul. This, however, has not restrained scholars from speculating. As G. Walter Hansen notes, the agitators have been "identified as Jewish Christians, Gentile Christians, non-Christian Jews . . . Judaizers, syncretistic Jewish Christians, Gnostic Jewish Christians . . . envoys of the Jerusalem apostles, and/or competitors of the Jerusalem apostles"[1] and more. The vast number of proposals,[2] many of which contradict each other, should serve as a warning as to the methodological hazards of reconstructing a historical situation from a vantage point some 2,000 years after the event.

The problem is nevertheless a real one. Paul never identifies his opponents, nor systematically describes their teaching, and the text of Galatians simply contains Paul's admonishments to the Galatian believers, not his systematic response to his agitators. So while Paul's heated letter to the Galatians doubtless contains many helpful (and trustworthy) details of the situation, a full reconstruction of the beliefs of the agitators is methodologically impossible. Ideally, one would be able to establish three different positions: "(1) how the opponents understood them [the issues], (2) how the Galatian Christians understood them, and (3) how Paul understood them."[3] From the letter itself one can sketch a likely scenario regarding Paul's understanding of the problems in the Galatian church. But it is virtually impossible to fill in the details of the opponents' teaching.

Some have suggested it is possible to reconstruct the basic positions of Paul's opponents by reversing Paul's claims. "Simply to reverse Paul's affirmations is at times helpful in gaining a handle on what the opponents taught and why they taught as they did. At other times, [however], it may reflect more how the Galatian Christians understood matters."[4] There is no method, including the reversing of Paul's affirmations, that can paint a certain and complete picture of the first-century situation. So, while it is necessary to practice some form of "mirror reading"—reading back through Galatians in an attempt to determine the identity and beliefs of Paul's opponents—this procedure must be done cautiously. Such an exer-

---

[1] G. Walter Hansen, *Abraham in Galatians: Epistolary and Rhetorical Contexts, JSNT* Sup Series 29 (Sheffield: JSOT, 1989), 167.
[2] See the bibliography of works regarding Paul's opponents in Galatia in Richard Longe-necker, *Galatians,* Word Biblical Commentary (Dallas, Tex.: Word, 1990), lxxxiii-lxxxix. Especially note John M. G. Barclay, "Mirror-Reading a Polemical Letter: Galatians as a Test Case," *Journal for the Study of the New Testament* 31 (1987): 73-93. Also, most works on Galatians have a section on this issue. For example, see Hansen, *Abraham in Galatians,* 167-174; or In-Gyu Hong, *The Law in Galatians, JSNT* Sup Series 81 (Sheffield: JSOT, 1993), 110-120.
[3] Longenecker, *Galatians,* lxxxix.
[4] Ibid.

cise is difficult, and the speculative nature of conclusions derived by utilizing "mirror reading" should be acknowledged at the onset.

Having expressed a necessary measure of caution regarding such methodology, we can nevertheless move forward in search of an understanding of the situation in Galatia. The most reliable source of information for this task is found in the letter itself.[5] What does the Galatian letter reveal concerning Paul's opponents? Some agitators (5:12) had come into the community and had thrown the Galatians into confusion (1:7). They taught, among other things, that the Galatians must be circumcised (5:2-3; 6:12). In addition, these opponents had been circumcised themselves so as to avoid persecution for the cross of Christ (6:12).

The teaching of the opponents must have persuaded many, for Paul described the Galatian believers as "turning to a different gospel" (1:6), one that was a perversion of "the gospel of Christ" (1:7). Paul's reference to a "different gospel" appears to imply that the Galatians knew the true gospel. The reference in 1:6-7 to the gospel, then, coupled with the reference to the cross of Christ in 6:12, reveal that the opponents considered themselves Christians. Paul, however, adamantly rejected the false gospel being propagated, thereby implying he believed that these agitators were, in fact, *not* Christians.

Other inferences may be drawn from the letter. It is possible that Paul was not personally familiar with his opponents in Galatia. "He refers to them generally as 'some people' . . . and 'anybody'. . . in his opening statement of the problem (1:7-9); he asks during the course of his treatment such questions as 'Who has bewitched you?' (3:1) and 'Who cut in on you and kept you from obeying the truth?' (5:7); and he

---

[5] If one is committed to a divinely inspired, authoritative text, a concomitant belief is that the text itself contains what is essential to understand it. Efforts to understand Galatians that *begin* with an assessment of Judaism at this time, or a theology of the agitators as determined from extra-biblical sources, are misguided not only methodologically, but theologically as well. Caneday comments, "Paul provides an authorized perspective upon the [Galatian] crisis and he invites the exegete simply to 'read over his shoulder' without searching for an 'objective' viewpoint. Therefore, Paul's invitation to read over his shoulder imposes certain expectations upon the reader. Understanding of the *Sitz im Leben* and purpose of the letter must not be done from a detached posture of historical objectivity. Concern for the *Sitz im Leben* of Galatians does not get its bearings from historical theoretics but from Christian theological interest in Paul's authorized perspective. *Such a posture of submission to Paul's perspective as preserved by divine inspiration must govern the evidence. . . .*" (final italics mine). Ardel B. Caneday, "The Curse of the Law and the Cross: Works of the Law and Faith in Galatians 3:1-14" (Ph.D. dissertation, Trinity Evangelical Divinity School, 1992), 61.

warns, 'The one who is throwing you into confusion will pay the penalty, whoever he may be' (5:10). . . ."[6]

It is also likely that Paul's opponents were Jewish. His extended explanation of the purpose and function of the law,[7] the use of Abraham in his arguments, his references to Sarah and Hagar and Jerusalem, and his mention of Jewish practices regarding circumcision, table manners, and observation of special days, all imply that Paul was engaging Jewish opposition. Perhaps the strongest indication that his opponents were Jewish is found in 6:12: "Those who want to make a good impression outwardly are trying to compel you to be circumcised."

From the text of the letter itself, then, it seems relatively certain that Paul's opponents were Jewish "Christians" who were teaching, in part, that the Galatians needed to be circumcised (6:12) and observe special days, months, seasons, and years (4:10). They had "cut in" on Paul's teaching (5:7) and were successfully causing many to abandon his teaching for "another gospel" (1:6).

Once it has been determined that the opponents were Jewish "Christians," it is necessary to learn as much as possible about their teaching. What was it about the agitators' message that so aroused Paul's wrath, causing him to label their teaching a *different* gospel? What was the essence of the Galatian problem?

Galatians itself provides many clues as to the specific situation. Many of the Galatians, in confusion, were deserting Christ and turning to a "different gospel" (1:6-7). They had received the Spirit by "believing what [they] heard" (3:2), and had run "a good race" up to that point (5:7), but now they were "trying to attain [their] goal by human effort" (3:3). Although they knew God (4:8), many were turning back "to those weak and miserable principles" that previously enslaved them (4:9). Evidently some wanted to be under the law again (4:9, 21) and had begun to observe special days, months, seasons, and years (4:10). They

---

[6] Longenecker, *Galatians*, xciv.

[7] The term νόμος (law) is used thirty-two times in Galatians. While Paul can use the term to denote various concepts, the overwhelming majority of his uses in Galatians are tied in some way to the Mosaic law. "Paul uses *nomos* most often and most basically of the Mosaic law." Douglas J. Moo, "'Law,' 'Works of the Law,' and 'Legalism' in Paul," *Westminster Theological Journal* 45 (1983): 80. Exceptions in Galatians include at least 3:21 ("if a law had been given that could impart life . . .") and 6:2 ("Carry each other's burdens, and in this way you will fulfill the law of Christ."). In addition to Moo, see Thomas Schreiner, *The Law and Its Fulfillment* (Grand Rapids, Mich.: Baker, 1993), 33-40.

were being pressured to be circumcised (5:3; 6:12-13, 15), causing Paul to warn them against any attempt to be justified by the law (5:4). Sadly, the Galatians had lost their joy and now doubted Paul (4:15-16). The poisonous influence of the agitators in Galatia was of great concern to Paul, and the intensity of his rebuttal (1:9-10; 5:12) shows his awareness of the critical nature of what was transpiring in the Galatian church.

Given the details of the situation provided in the letter, one might conclude that scholars would generally agree on the basics of the problem Paul sought to address. This has not been the case. From the same pieces of information, numerous vastly different proposals have been put forth as to the major problem in Galatia. As a result, radically different assessments of Paul's message have been suggested. Surveying all the different analyses of the Galatian situation is impossible in this work, yet it is important to investigate those issues that bear upon Galatians 3:28. We will briefly examine two of the most important and controversial issues.

### The Problem: Getting In or Staying In?

Were Paul's opponents teaching salvation through the "works of the law," or were they insisting that those who were already believers, especially Gentiles, should keep the law? Were they teaching both? Sometimes this question is stated as follows: Were Paul's opponents teaching that the works of the law are necessary for "getting in" or that they were necessary for "staying in"? E. P. Sanders contends, "The argument of Galatians 3 . . . is against the view that Gentiles must accept the law *as a condition* of or as a basic requirement for membership."[8] For Sanders, Galatians 3 is about how one "enters the people of God"[9] and the entire argument of Galatians 3–4 is "that righteousness was never, in God's plan, intended to be by the law."[10] God's people have never been justified by the "works of the law," regardless of how one defines this term, which is why Paul must attack any position that teaches this.

Certainly Sanders is correct when he asserts that the Galatian opponents must have taught that works of the law were necessary for "get-

---

[8] E. P. Sanders, *Paul, the Law, and the Jewish People* (Philadelphia: Fortress, 1983), 19, italics his.
[9] Ibid.
[10] Ibid., 27.

ting in." Galatians 2:15-16 and 2:21 strongly affirm that justification is never by the works of the law, and Paul emphatically returns to this truth again in 3:10-14. It is difficult to understand why Paul would mention justification by works if it had not been a problem in Galatia. Furthermore, the fact that Paul's opponents insisted upon circumcision is additional evidence that the issue of "getting in" was being disputed. While it is probable that the agitators would have pressured Gentiles "already in" to be circumcised, it is more reasonable to assume that they demanded circumcision as a requirement to "get in." Even though circumcision originally was established as a sign of God's gracious covenant (Gen. 17:9ff.) and not as a "work," it is easy to understand how it could be perceived as a meritorious act, especially for uncircumcised Gentiles. If the Gentiles were not circumcised, it might be argued, they could not be God's people. Hence, circumcision could easily be seen as a "work of the law" necessary for salvation. These evidences show that the Galatian problem involved a dispute over justification—"getting in."

Longenecker and others, however, argue that the Galatian agitators also taught that works of the law were necessary for sanctification as well as justification. Sanders is wrong, they argue, when he limits Paul's critique of the works of the law to the issue of how one becomes a member of God's people. Paul criticized his opponents because they insisted that the works of the law were important for both "getting in" *and* "staying in." Longenecker sees both of these emphases clearly revealed in 2:15-21: "The first [argument] in vv. 15-16, which he [Paul] believes is agreed to by all true believers, is that the law plays no positive role in becoming a Christian (contra 'legalism'). . . . The second is in vv. 17-20, where he argues that the law plays no positive role in Christian living (contra 'nomism') but rather the Christian life is lived 'in Christ.'"[11] Colin Kruse agrees with Longenecker, seeing both issues, justification and sanctification, addressed in Galatians. He also adopts Longenecker's twofold terminology of legalism and nomism. "Legalism" describes the view that works of the law are necessary for salvation. "Nomism" describes the belief that "those who have been justified by faith were required to observe the demands of the law as part of their ongoing

---

[11] Longenecker, *Galatians*, 82-83.

Christian obedience."[12] Kruse and Longenecker assert that *both* issues, legalism and nomism, are part of the Galatian problem.

If one begins with a reading of Galatians, without preconceived notions regarding what might be possible given the nature of Judaism at that time, it is fairly evident that both problems—"getting in" and "staying in"—are issues in Galatia. Concerning Paul's dispute with Peter in Antioch, which set up the theological arguments of Galatians 3–4, Paul says that he and Peter were in agreement concerning legalism—justification is by faith, not by the works of the law (2:15-16). They disagreed, however, on the issue of nomism—whether or not Peter should *live* like a Jew. Paul restates this in 2:19, where he writes, "Through the law I died to the law so that I might *live* for God." Paul is concerned about how the law relates to his daily Christian experience.

Paul addresses both legalism and nomism in 3:1-5 as well. He begins by pointing to the Galatians' initial justification/reception of the Spirit, assuming it is self-evident to all that the initial experience was based on faith, not on works of the law (contra legalism). He then argues from the Galatians' initial salvation experience to their present Christian life; the central message in 3:1-5 deals with nomism—how the works of the law relate to the Christian life.

Numerous other indications in the letter confirm that the Galatians, as Christians, were struggling with the role of the law in their ongoing Christian lives. For example: "But now that you know God— or rather are known by God—how is it that you are *turning back* to those weak and miserable principles?" (4:9); "You *were* running a good race. Who cut in on you and kept you from obeying the truth?" (5:7); "It is for freedom that Christ has set us free. Stand firm, then, and do not let yourselves be burdened *again* by a yoke of slavery" (5:1; emphasis added in all three references). There are other examples, but these are sufficient to conclude that the Galatian problem involved both "getting in" and "staying in." Whatever the agitators were teaching, and however one interprets "works of the law," it is clear that both issues were involved.

---

[12] Colin G. Kruse, *Paul, the Law, and Justification* (Leicester, England: Apollos, 1996), 69.

### The Problem with the "Works of the Law"

The phrase "works of the law"[13] appears only six times in Galatians (2:16 [3x]; 3:2, 5, 10, NASB; NIV, "observing the law"), but the concept is quite important in the letter. Works of the law, Paul argues, do not justify one before God; rather, justification is by faith in Jesus Christ (2:16).[14] The logical implication is that the Galatian opponents had taught the opposite, that works of the law were somehow essential for justification. Five of the six occurrences of "works of the law" are clearly related to the issue of justification (2:16 [3x], 3:2, 10). The use in 3:5, however, ties this phrase with the ongoing Christian life (contra nomism): "Does He then, who provides you [present participle] with the Spirit and works miracles [present participle] among you, do it by the works of the law, or by hearing with faith?" (NASB). The Galatian problem, as previously shown, involved both "getting in" and "staying in," and the dispute revolved in part around how works of the law related to both justification and the ongoing Christian life.

The meaning of the phrase "works of the law" is important, and hotly contested. Some, such as Moo,[15] Schreiner,[16] Kruse,[17] Westerholm,[18] and Longenecker,[19] see "works of the law" as simply works required by the Old Testament law. The Old Testament, and Judaism, did not necessarily teach that the works of the law could justify one before God, but Paul's opponents evidently did. Others, such as Cranfield[20] and Fuller,[21] see "works of the law" as legalistic works done out of a distorted view of the Old Testament. Nothing is suspect regarding the Old Testament law, according to this view—Paul simply criticizes

---

[13] Gk. ἔργων νόμου

[14] There is a growing number of scholars who interpret πίστεως Ἰησοῦ Χριστοῦ as a subjective genitive, "the faith/faithfulness of Jesus Christ." The traditional interpretation has been to view this as an objective genitive, "faith in Jesus Christ." Though this is doubtless an important issue, it is not within the scope of this work, for one's position on this issue is not critical to the interpretation of Galatians 3:28. See the summary in Joseph Fitzmeyer, *Romans: A New Translation with Introduction and Commentary,* The Anchor Bible Series (New York: Doubleday, 1993), 345-346.

[15] Moo, "'Law,' 'Works of the Law,' and 'Legalism' in Paul," 92.

[16] Schreiner, *The Law,* 52.

[17] Kruse, *Paul,* 68.

[18] Stephen Westerholm, *Israel's Law and the Church's Faith* (Grand Rapids, Mich.: Eerdmans, 1988), 120-121.

[19] Longenecker, *Galatians,* 86.

[20] C. E. B. Cranfield, "St. Paul and the Law," *Scottish Journal of Theology* 17 (1964): 43-68.

[21] Daniel. P. Fuller, "Paul and 'The Works of the Law'," *Westminster Theological Journal* 38 (1975–76): 28-42.

a *misuse* of it. And, in fact, in this view any works/faith contrast is artificial and mistaken, as both works *and* faith are important in both the
Old and New Testaments. Others, such as Luther[22] and Bultmann,[23] see
"works of the law" as any human endeavor that attempts to amass merit
in the sight of God, not just works related to the law. These scholars note
that the principle of "law" is directly tied to "doing." Hence, Paul is contrasting the principle of law/doing with that of faith. *Any* attempt to justify oneself, whether it be through works of the Old Testament law or
in other ways, is wrong. Dunn[24] sees "works of the law" as being deeds
the law requires, but specifically those works that were Jewish identity
markers, such as circumcision and Jewish table customs. What Paul is
denying is that Jews are justified because of their national identity markers and covenant privileges. For Dunn, the contrast is not works versus
faith but Jewish nationalism versus Gentile. Many other views could be
mentioned as well.

While the debate over the meaning of "works of the law" is critical
in its own right, we will focus on the implications of the definition of
this expression that are pertinent for our study.

First, as has already been shown, the Galatian problem involved
false teaching regarding the works of the law and their importance for
*both* justification *and* the ongoing Christian life. The works of the law,
says Paul, are not necessary for either.

Second, it is important to recognize that, regardless of how one
defines "the works of the law," *these works are Jewish* in Galatians.
Dunn and Sanders are right when they assert that the works of the law
in Galatians are primarily the "identity markers" of circumcision,
observing special calendar events, and table fellowship. These are, after
all, the specific issues Paul mentions. It is possible, and indeed likely, that
works of the law are doomed because they are "works," and not specif-

---

[22] Martin Luther, *A Commentary on St. Paul's Epistle to the Galatians* (Westwood, N.J.: Fleming
H. Revell, 1953), 145. Luther said, "*No monk shall be justified by his order, no nun by her
chastity, no citizen by his probity, no prince by his beneficence, & c.* The law of God is greater
than the whole world, for it comprehendeth all men, and the works of the law do far excel even
the most glorious will-works of all the merit-mongers; and yet Paul saith that neither the law nor
the works of the law do justify. Therefore we conclude with Paul, that faith only justifieth" (italics original).
[23] See summary of Bultmann on this topic in Westerholm, *Israel's Law*, 70–75.
[24] James D. G. Dunn, *Jesus, Paul and the Law: Studies in Mark and Galatians* (Louisville, Ky.:
Westminster/John Knox, 1990), 215–236.

ically because they are of "the law."[25] This seems to be implied by 3:10b, and, if this is the case, Paul would find fault with all "works," whether they are of the law or not. In fact, in Romans 4:4-5 Paul affirms that God justifies the one "who does not work"; so clearly works, regardless of their nature, fail to justify. But in Galatians the main focus is on works tied to the law. Whether these works are unable to justify because they are Jewish, or because Christ has inaugurated another way of salvation, or because they are merit-amassing works and not faith, is an important question, but not for our purposes. What is, however, necessary for our purposes is the recognition that the Galatian problem involved Jewish works of some form or another.

Third, the expression "works of the law" (or "observing the law"), when it is presented in contrast with something else, always appears in opposition to expressions involving "faith."[26] Here are the six uses of the phrase "works of the law"[27] in Galatians:

|       | Not *"works of the law" but . . .* | The result |
|-------|-----------------------------------|------------|
| 2:16  | "by faith in Jesus Christ"[28]    | justification |
| 2:16  | "by faith in Christ"[29]          | justification |
| 2:16  | (no contrast made)                |            |
| 3:2   | "by believing what you heard"[30] | receive the Spirit |
| 3:5   | "believe what you heard"[31]      | God gives Spirit/ works miracles |
| 3:10  | (no contrast made)                |            |

Note that "works of the law" is contrasted with an expression containing the term "faith" and a reference (or allusion) to Christ. In 3:2 and 3:5 the contrasting expression "by believing what you heard" doesn't contain the word "Christ," but Christ is surely the implied object of belief. Paul is not contrasting works of the law with believing *anything* that was heard; rather, he is contrasting works of the law with believing what was heard

---

[25] Douglas J. Moo, "Paul and the Law in the Last Ten Years," *Scottish Journal of Theology* 40 (1987): 298.
[26] Gk. πίστις
[27] Gk. ἔργων νόμου
[28] Gk. διὰ πίστεως Ἰησοῦ Χριστοῦ
[29] Gk. ἐκ πίστεως Χριστοῦ
[30] Gk. ἐξ ἀκοῆς πίστεως
[31] Gk. ἐξ ἀκοῆς πίστεως

about Christ. Traditionally, scholars have emphasized the "works/faith" contrast in Galatians, and rightly so, as this is an important part of Paul's argument. But the contrast between the law and Christ is also noteworthy, as will become evident below. It is sufficient at this point to note that the elusive "works of the law" are contrasted with expressions incorporating the concept of faith *and* the person and work of Christ.

Though much remains to be said regarding the works of the law, it is important for this study to note that these works are Jewish, they involve both "getting in" and "staying in," and they are contrasted with faith and Christ.

### The Galatian Problem: A Proposal

It is now possible to offer a reasonable suggestion as to the nature of the Galatian problem: Jewish "Christians," personally unknown to Paul, were subverting the true gospel by teaching that Gentiles must submit to the Old Testament law, specifically the identity markers of circumcision, calendar observance, and rules of table fellowship, in order to be justified and continue on in their Christian life. In other words, the opponents taught that Jewish works of the law were necessary for the Gentiles to "get in" and to "remain in." These agitators proclaimed a "different gospel," a gospel requiring the works of the law, from beginning to end.

Behind the agitators' teaching, however, loomed a larger question, one that Paul recognized as underlying the presenting problem: Given the Jewish roots of the gospel—the inheritance promised through Abraham, the law, and now, the arrival of a Jewish Messiah—how are Gentiles to be incorporated into this Jewish story? Do the Gentile Galatians need to become Jewish or become affiliated with the law-covenant in order to become part of God's people?

Beneath these questions lies an even more fundamental issue: How does the arrival of the promised Christ, and the new covenant with the Spirit, change the old? Or, put another way: If the locus of God's salvific activity in years past was the nation Israel, with her God-given promises and law, what has changed, both for the Jew and for the Gentile, now that the new covenant and the Spirit have arrived and the focus of God's salvific activity is no longer tribally based?

It is important to recognize at the onset that the Galatian problem, in Paul's mind, was much more serious than who can eat with whom. Larger theological meta-questions govern Paul's answers. While Paul's initial comments were provoked by specific situations regarding table customs and circumcision, he formulates his responses to these issues from broader salvation-historical[32] realities. The situations in Antioch and Galatia came about because many in the early church failed to grasp the changes that resulted from the arrival of Christ and the new covenant. The dangerously distorted teaching of the Jewish "Christian" agitators—that works of the law are necessary for the Gentiles to "get in" and to "stay in"—provided Paul an ideal opportunity to clarify how God, in the fullness of time, used Israel and the promises given to Abraham to bless all nations with his Son and Spirit.

The Galatian problem, then, can be summarized as twofold. There are *presenting problems* such as the pressure to be circumcised (6:12) and to observe special days, months, seasons, and years (4:10). Then there is the foundational *theological problem:* How does the arrival of Christ, and the new covenant, affect the old? Because answers to the first set of problems are found in the answer to the second theological problem, Paul devotes his energy to addressing the second issue. It is within his answer to this second question that Galatians 3:28 appears.

## PAUL'S ARGUMENT IN GALATIANS 2:15–3:29

Given a working assessment of the Galatian problem, we must now examine how Paul crafts his response to the problem. Most interpreters note that Paul's report of the conflict in Antioch (2:11-14) spawned his extended theological argument as presented in 2:15ff. As Paul explains, Peter, a Jew, was eating with Gentiles until some men from James came (2:12). At that time Peter withdrew from his Gentile brethren and, in light of his fear of the "circumcision group," even began to force these Gentiles to follow Jewish customs (2:12-14). The incident itself raised many questions: How should Jewish believers, those from God's chosen nation, relate to those believers who were on the "outside"—the Gentile "sinners"? Were Jewish believers to shun Gentile believers if they refused to follow Jewish table customs? Should Gentile believers be required to keep Jewish customs and the Old Testament law, especially circumci-

---

[32] More will be said below about "salvation-history."

sion? These particular questions, flowing out of the Antioch dispute, were doubtless a concern for Paul as he set forth his response in Galatians 2:15ff. It would be a mistake, however, to assume that the Antioch dispute was of utmost importance to Paul.

What *was* most important to Paul? What are the broader theological issues that shaped Paul's response as crafted in Galatians 3–4? Working from the parts to the whole, one could begin by examining, paragraph by paragraph, each individual thought unit in Paul's response contained in Galatians 3–4. After dissecting the parts, a proposal could be made regarding the whole. This approach, while it has the advantage of focusing in on the immediate context, runs the risk of missing the broader themes of Galatians. For example, Paul's short paragraph on the purpose of the law (3:19-20) can be carefully analyzed (albeit with great difficulty), but even with an accurate interpretation of 3:19-20, one must ask why Paul chose to address the issue of "the law" at all. The word *law*[33] doesn't appear in the letter until 2:15; it is likely that Paul had other concerns in mind than solely a discourse on the law.

A second approach, better suited for Galatians 3–4, is to glance first at central themes woven throughout the book, and then focus on the parts. This approach has the potential pitfall that one might illegitimately read emphases from elsewhere in the book into particular sections of Galatians 3–4. Yet it has the advantage of interpreting the parts within the whole of the letter. Thus, before we examine each individual section of Paul's argument, it will be most helpful to first explore a central, reoccurring theme found throughout the book, though most notably in chapters 3 and 4. Without an understanding of this theme—*the progress of God's redemptive plan throughout history*—it is impossible to appreciate Paul's teaching in Galatians 3:28.

### The Central Place of Salvation-History in Galatians 3–4

Paul's argument in Galatians 3–4 is founded on the progression of salvation-history.[34] Four particular observations reveal that this is the case.

---

[33] Gk. νόμος

[34] The term *salvation-history* has been used differently by various biblical scholars. Some, such as Rudolf Bultmann, use the term to denote "the interior, psychological, or existential response to God's dealings with his people through the centuries, apart from the actual historical phenomena which the Bible claims grounded the faith of biblical characters." Robert W. Yarbrough, "Heilsgeschichte," in *Evangelical Dictionary of Theology*, 2d ed., ed. Walter Elwell (Grand Rapids,

First, Paul repeatedly rests his case upon temporal evidence, for example, "But when the time had fully come . . ." Second, there are many salvation-historical concepts used throughout his argument. Third, many events predicted in the Old Testament, such as the arrival of the promised Spirit, are mentioned in Galatians 3–4 as having been fulfilled. Fourth, Christ's death is presented as a *means* to something new. In other words, the arrival of Christ, and his death and resurrection, have ushered in something new.

Let's look at the evidence for each of these four observations concerning Paul's emphasis on salvation-history in Galatians 3–4.

i) Given the situational nature of the Galatian letter, it is striking the number of times Paul makes temporal, salvation-historical references in his response to the specific Galatian problem. Especially noteworthy are the preponderance of these terms in chapters 3–4 (all italics mine):

1:4       "Jesus Christ, who gave himself . . . to rescue us from the present evil *age.*"

3:8       "The Scripture *foresaw*[35] that God would justify the Gentiles by faith, and announced the gospel *in advance*[36] to Abraham."

3:17      "The law, introduced 430 years *later,* does not set aside the covenant *previously established*[37] by God."

3:19      "It [the law] was added because of transgressions *until* the Seed to whom the promise referred had come."

---

Mich.: Baker, forthcoming). In other words, the historicity of biblical events is not important. What is important, however, is the inner, existential response to these "events." In distinction to Bultmann's salvation-history, Oscar Cullman, George Eldon Ladd, and others have used the term to denote *the progression of historical events and persons through which God reveals and accomplishes his redemptive activity.* According to this view, there is no radical distinction between history and salvation. On the contrary, the Scriptures themselves, both OT and NT, point to real events and people as the means by which God reveals and accomplishes redemption. Salvation-history is portrayed as progressive; one event builds on another, and past events are further clarified and illumined by more recent events. Cullman comments, "In the origin of biblical salvation history, we are therefore dealing with a kind of *chain* of salvation-historical insights and representations in which each time a new event and a new revelation about it are aligned with the previous revelation, so that the previous revelation is at the same time placed in a new perspective." Oscar Cullman, *Salvation in History,* trans. Sidney Sowers and others (New York: Harper & Row, 1965), 91. In this work, the expression "salvation-history" will refer to the chain of biblical, historical events through which God progressively reveals and accomplishes his redemptive plan.
[35] Gk. προεῖδον
[36] Gk. προευαγγελίζομαι
[37] Gk. προκυρόω

3:22    "The whole world is a prisoner of sin, so that what was promised
        . . . *might be given*[38] to those who believe."
3:23    "*Before* this faith came, we were held prisoners by the law,
        locked up *until faith should be revealed.*"[39]
3:25    "Now that faith *has come,* we are no longer under the supervi-
        sion of the law."
4:2     "He is subject to guardians and trustees *until the time* set by his
        father."
4:3-4   "We *were* in slavery . . . but *when the time had fully come,* God
        sent his Son, born of a woman, born under law."[40]
6:15    "Neither circumcision nor uncircumcision means anything; what
        counts is a *new* creation."

It is clear that Paul viewed the arrival of the present time—the time
of Christ, in distinction to the past—as an important part of his argument. "Before this faith [Christ] came," Paul notes, certain things were
true; "now that faith [Christ] has come" other things are true (3:23-25).

ii) In addition to these temporal references, it is clear from Paul's
choice of terms that salvation-history is important for his argument.
Terms such as *promise* (3:14, 16, 17, 18 [2x], 21, 22, 29; 4:23, 28),
*heir/inheritance* (3:18, 29; 4:1, 7, 30; 5:21), *blessed/blessing* (3:8, 9, 14),
and *covenant* (3:15, 17; 4:24) have, over the history of redemption,
become laden with salvation-historical implications. Paul could have
addressed the Antioch problem without using these terms. He utilizes
them in his argument, however, because these concepts are necessary to
explain his answer to the particular Galatian situation.

iii) Not only does Paul utilize salvation-historical concepts, he
affirms the present fulfillment of at least three promised events that were
linked to the arrival of the new covenant. In Joel 2:28ff. God promised
to "pour out my Spirit on all people." In Galatians 4:4ff. Paul declares
that this promise has now been fulfilled. Second, throughout the Old

---

[38] Gk. δοθῇ, subjunctive
[39] Gk. τὴν μέλλουσαν πίστιν ἀποκαλυφθῆναι
[40] Gk. ἦλθεν τὸ πλήρωμα τοῦ χρόνου

Testament it is clear that the Gentiles will one day be included as part of God's people (e.g., Gen. 12:3). Now Paul states that both Jews and Gentiles are heirs of Abraham through Christ (Gal. 3:26-29). God's people are no longer primarily a nation, but are known, both Jew and Gentile, by virtue of being in Christ. And, a third long anticipated event (Isa. 58:13-14; Jer. 12:14-15) is the reception of the promised inheritance. Paul states that now, through Christ, those who belong to him can actually receive the promise (3:29; 4:7).

iv) Finally, the centrality of the salvation-historical theme is seen in how Christ's death and crucifixion is presented as a *means* to accomplish what had previously been promised. This is clearly seen by examining two purpose clauses[41] in Galatians 3 and 4. Note:

> [Christ] redeemed us *in order that* the blessing given to Abraham might come to the Gentiles . . . *so that* by faith we might receive the promise of the Spirit. (3:14)

> God sent his son . . . to redeem those under the law, *that* we might receive the full rights of sons. (4:4-5)

Paul describes Christ's death as the *means* by which the Gentiles received the blessings of Abraham, the promised Spirit was given, and the status of full sonship was procured. In other words, the time of Christ ushered in something new, which had been promised long ago.

Paul's argument throughout Galatians 3–4 is predicated upon changes in redemptive history brought about by the arrival of Christ, and consequently, the new covenant. Specific issues in Galatians 3–4, whether it be the role of the law or the right to be a child of Abraham, must be seen in light of the progress of, and changes in, redemptive history. For example, Paul deals with the issues of legalism and nomism, which were doubtless critical problems for the Galatian church, by pointing to salvation-historical realities. For Paul "the fullness of time has been entered upon and the new creation has dawned with the advent

---

[41] Gk. ἵνα

of Christ. . . . The fullness of time takes effect with the sending of God's Son, born of a woman, born under the law (Gal. 4:4)."[42] The new has broken in upon the old, and although this new age is in some manner continuous with the old, nevertheless it is an overwhelming and decisive transition to a new world and a new covenant.[43] Christ's death and resurrection, and the arrival of the Spirit, shine new light on previous salvation-history, including the requirements of the Sinai legislation, the Promise, God's redemptive activity as focused primarily on Israel, and the status of those who were children of Abraham. With the arrival of Christ (Gal. 3:23, 25) and the subsequent inauguration of the new aeon, the "old" must be reassessed, including issues such as circumcision, the law, Jewish relationships with Gentiles, and how Gentiles relate to the promise made to Abraham.

It is necessary to highlight the significance of salvation-history in Paul's argument in Galatians 3–4, for without an appreciation of this foundation it is not possible to understand how, and why, he argues on specific issues such as the purpose of the law. It is also crucial for the purposes of this work to note that Galatians 3:28, far from being an isolated saying regarding oneness or male/female relationships, occurs at a climactic point in Paul's extended description of salvation-history. Galatians 3:28, then, must be interpreted in such a manner as to fit within Paul's larger salvation-historical argument as developed in Galatians 3–4.

### The Function of Each Thought Unit in 2:15–3:29[44]

Having highlighted Paul's emphasis on salvation-history, we must now summarize succinctly each specific thought unit leading up to and including Galatians 3:26-29, especially noting those issues that bear upon the interpretation of 3:28. Many important, and controversial, issues will be passed over in this summary if they are tangential to understanding 3:28.

---

[42] Herman Ridderbos, *Paul: An Outline of His Theology*, trans. John Richard De Witt (Grand Rapids, Mich.: Eerdmans, 1975), 54.

[43] Ibid., 55.

[44] It is difficult to know at what point Paul transitions out of his salvation-historical argument. Surely redemptive history plays a major role in his thinking at least through the end of chapter 4. And certainly there is a close tie between 3:26-29 and 4:1-7 (both sections deal with sonship, inheritance, and Christ). Yet, for the purposes of this thesis, I will summarize 2:15–3:29, rather than all of chapters 3–4.

## GALATIANS 2:15-21

Betz,[45] Longenecker,[46] and others have argued that these verses summarize the earlier content of Galatians and introduce the arguments that are to follow. Paul affirms that he and Peter agree that works of the law are in no way necessary for justification (2:15-16). In 2:17ff., however, Paul turns to discuss the role of the law in his daily Christian experience. From his argumentative style, it appears that Peter and Paul disagreed about this issue, at least on this occasion regarding this particular situation. Paul argues that he has died to the law, having been crucified with Christ, so that his ongoing Christian experience is characterized by faith in Christ, who lives in him, and not by the law. In 2:21 he summarizes his argument with an emphatic negation, stating that Christ's death, by the grace of God, renders even the possibility of righteousness through the law ridiculous.

Several themes appear in 2:15-21 that will reappear later, including the relationship of the law and "works of the law" to "getting in" (vv. 15-16) and "staying in" (vv. 17-20); the centrality of Christ's death (vv. 19, 20, 21); the apparent tension between the law and Christ (vv. 19-20, 21); and the Jew/Gentile question (v. 15). In the verses that follow Paul presents several different arguments that address these issues.

## GALATIANS 3:1-6

Paul begins his first argument with an appeal to the experience of the Galatians: "Did you receive the Spirit by observing the law, or by believing what you heard? Are you so foolish? After beginning with the Spirit, are you now trying to attain your goal by human effort?" (3:2b-3). It is an accepted fact, Paul argues, that the Galatians began their Christian experience by faith, rather than by the works of the law. Likewise, he argues, God presently works in their lives through their believing what is heard, not through the "works of the law" (3:5, NASB). The pronoun change to "you" in this section is significant; Paul has transitioned from personal reflections on his daily experience with the law to directly addressing the Galatians.

---

[45] H. D. Betz, *A Commentary on Paul's Epistle to the Galatians,* Hermenia (Philadelphia: Fortress, 1979), 113ff.
[46] Longenecker, *Galatians,* 80-81.

The appeal to Abraham as an example (3:6ff.) has caused confusion among interpreters: Is 3:6 to be read with 3:5, or does 3:6 begin a new thought?[47] Actually, 3:6 serves as a hinge, linking what has gone before with what follows and should be read with what precedes *and* what follows.[48] Thus, as a summary to 3:1-5, Abraham, the consummate Jewish example of righteousness, serves as a weighty example of one who was justified by faith, not by obedience to the law.

GALATIANS 3:6-9

Abraham, as an exemplary man of faith, served as the perfect conclusion for Paul's first argument in 3:1-5, but now in what follows (3:6ff.), Abraham plays a much more foundational role in Paul's case. This second argument, contained in 3:6-9, is much different than his first. Rather than appealing to the experience of the Galatians, he crafts his argument by appealing to Scripture and points the Galatians to their forefather in faith, Abraham. First, Abraham is portrayed as the representative head ("through you,"[49] 3:8), which sets the stage for Paul's teaching that Christ is now the representative head ("in Christ Jesus," 3:26ff.) of all God's people. Abraham is important, not simply as a role model of faith, but because he is the forerunner of the ultimate Head of God's people. Second, by appealing to the statement about Abraham in Genesis 15:6, and to the fact that the initial promise given to him foresaw the inclusion of the Gentiles (Gal. 3:8), Paul lays the foundation for his claim that now Gentiles are included in God's people (3:28). Third, the reference to Abraham doubtless elicited thoughts among faithful Jews of one day becoming heirs of the promise given to their forefather. Thus, the mention of Abraham sets the stage for Paul's later claim that the inheritance

---

[47] The NA 27 sets 3:6 off as the start of a new thought, while UBS 3 places 3:6 as the conclusion to 3:5. Williams argues 3:6 goes with 3:5. Part of his reasoning is that justification and the reception of the Spirit are often concomitant ideas in Galatians. Hence, 3:5, which mentions the Spirit, would likely be tied to 3:6, which talks about justification. "Justification and the Spirit: in Paul's mind one necessarily implies the other, and to claim the one without evidencing the other would misapprehend the Christian life." Sam Williams, "Justification of the Spirit in Galatians," *Journal for the Study of the New Testament* 29 (1987): 98.

[48] Longenecker agrees that this is probable: "The fact that καθώς has such a broad semantic range as to include use as a comparative, use with γέγραπται as an introductory formula, and use as an *exemplum* reference allows Paul to use it in a bridging fashion, signaling directly an *exemplum* argument but also setting up arguments from Scripture." Longenecker, *Galatians,* 112.

[49] Gk. ἐν σοὶ

is now available in the fullness of time, and that it consists of full rights as sons and possession of the Spirit of God's Son (4:5-6).

In summary, it is clear that Paul's reference to Abraham in 3:6-9 is crucial, far beyond his role as a model of faith, as it sets up many facets of his forthcoming argument.

## GALATIANS 3:10-14

3:10-14 is often viewed as an excursus, because without it Paul's teaching on Abraham would flow uninterrupted from 3:9 to 3:15-18. While it is true that Abraham exits the discussion at this point, it is erroneous to conclude that this paragraph is incidental to the argument. In fact, this paragraph provides the *why* and *how* of the first two arguments. *Why* do "works of the law" not justify (from 2:15-16; 3:1-5)? Answer: "All who rely on observing the law are under a curse" (3:10). *How* does the promised inheritance come from Abraham to the Gentiles (from 3:8-9)? Answer: "Christ redeemed us from the curse . . . in order that the blessing given to Abraham might come to the Gentiles" (3:13a, 14a). The two major themes revisited in 3:10-14—the contrast between observing the law and faith, and the promise made to Abraham—are not unrelated. They are bound together by the curse. Paul's third argument, then, ties the "works of the law" to a curse.

This paragraph has been the focal point of much of the recent debate over Paul and the law. The literature on it is overwhelming, but for our purposes, many of the most difficult questions may be sidestepped. Several points may be summarized. First, regardless of how one defines the problematic "works of the law," those who are of the "works of the law" are under a curse (3:10). Second, the curse is in force because people do not *do*[50] everything written in the law[51] (3:10). Third, Christ came at a specific time to redeem those under the curse (3:13). The curse was removed by Christ, through his death. Christ's death, then, is directly tied to the curse resulting from the "works of the law." Fourth, Christ redeemed those under the curse by becoming a curse for them (3:13). Here Paul notes the substitutionary importance of Christ's death ("for us"[52]). Finally, Christ is presented not only as the one who

---

[50] Gk. ποιῆσαι
[51] Gk. πᾶσιν τοῖς γεγραμμένοις ἐν τῷ βιβλίῳ
[52] Gk. ὑπὲρ ἡμῶν

removes the curse (3:13), but as the one who brings about the inclusion of the Gentiles (3:14a) and the arrival of the promised Spirit (3:14b).

To sum up Paul's arguments to this point: After reporting the Antioch incident (2:11-14), Paul turns to questions regarding how the "works of the law" relate to justification and sanctification (2:15-21). He first appeals to the Galatians' salvation experience (3:1-6), arguing that the "works of the law" did not produce conversion, nor will they produce Christian maturity. He points to Abraham as an example of one whose faith was credited to him as righteousness. He reminds them (3:6-9) that the gospel given to Abraham was by faith, and the blessings promised to Abraham flow out of faith. In addition (3:10-14), the "works of the law" are insufficient because of the curse: "Cursed is everyone who does not continue to do everything written in the Book of the Law" (3:10). The solution to this curse, and the remedy for those who have trusted in the "works of the law," is Christ. It is by faith in Christ that the blessings of Abraham flow to the Gentiles.

GALATIANS 3:15-18

Paul's fourth argument builds on his introduction of the concept of "promise" in 3:14b. Because the inheritance is based on a promise, the law cannot set it aside—because God gave the promise first (3:17). Previously Paul refuted the efficacy of the "works of the law," but now he addresses the role of the law itself. Paul uses a human analogy: Even a human covenant cannot be added to or subtracted from after it is ratified. In the same way, the promise cannot have the law added to it. If the inheritance is by the law, it cannot, by definition, be by a promise (3:18). But in fact the inheritance is by a promise, and the dominant theme for the next few paragraphs will be this promise and the relationship of God's law to God's promise.[53]

An additional point is important in this fourth argument. Paul states that the promises spoken to Abraham were intended for a singular recipient, Christ. This, doubtless, would have caused confusion, as earlier Paul said that the promised inheritance was for all "those who have faith . . . along with Abraham" (3:9). How can the promise be for one per-

---

[53] Note "promise" in 3:14, 16, 17, 18 (2x), 19, 21, 22, 29; 4:23, 28.

son and for many? The answer is revealed in 3:26-29, where those who
are in Christ (the many) are said to be Abraham's seed and heirs of the
promise because they are one in Christ (the one). More will be said on
this in our next chapter.

GALATIANS 3:19-22

This section is comprised of two paragraphs, each introduced by questions that logically flow from Paul's previous arguments. First (3:19-20),
if the inheritance always depended on a promise, what, then, is the purpose of the law? And, secondly (3:21-22), is the law, then, opposed to
God's promises? In some ways these two questions are an excursus; they
fail to directly advance Paul's argument. But these two brief paragraphs
do address important questions that have lingered since the beginning
of his discussion. Kruse comments,

> On the one hand, the passage is a digression in so far as it turns aside
> from the main flow of the argument running in the previous section. . . . On the other hand, the passage is not a digression in so far
> as it is central to Paul's main concerns in the letter as a whole, *i.e.* to
> combat not only legalism but also nomism. The present passage is crucial for achieving this, for in it Paul shows what the true function of
> the law was in salvation history.[54]

Paul's answers to the first question (3:19-20) are difficult, but two
points are clear. First, the law was *added* until Christ, to whom the
promise referred, had come. Hence, the Galatians should be looking to
Christ, not to the law. Second, whatever is meant by Paul's reference to
"angels," the effect of his statement in 3:20b is to downgrade "the law
in *comparison* to the promise."[55] The Galatians "should not be looking
to Moses and obedience to his law for their incorporation into the people of God, but rather looking to Christ and placing their faith in him."[56]

Regarding the second question (3:21-22), Paul absolutely denies
that God's law is opposed to God's promise. If the law could have provided life and righteousness, these things would have come by the law
(3:21). But this was impossible, because "the whole world is a prisoner

---

[54] Kruse, *Paul*, 91.
[55] Ibid., 92, italics mine.
[56] Ibid., 93.

of sin," and as a result the promise comes through faith in Christ, not through the works of the law (3:22).

## GALATIANS 3:23-25

Paul's final argument points to the role of the law now that Christ has come. While much has been said about the law, or works of the law, and Christ, the relationship between the two has been ambiguous. The expressions "before this faith came"[57] (3:23) and "now that faith has come"[58] (3:25) both refer to the arrival of Christ. Note the following about the law: i) it imprisons; ii) it is temporal (cf. 3:19); iii) its purpose is to lead us to Christ (3:24) so that we might be justified by faith (3:24)[59]; and, iv) with the arrival of Christ, believers are no longer under the law (3:25). Paul doesn't say Christ and the law are opposed to each other; rather, he says that the law precedes Christ and points to Christ. Now, with the arrival of Christ, believers are no longer under the supervision of the law (3:25).[60]

## GALATIANS 3:26-29

Although we will look at this passage extensively in the next chapter, several points are important here regarding the flow of Paul's argument. There is a major change in focus at 3:26, as indicated by the pronoun change back to *you*. This is the first time Paul has directly addressed his readers since the acerbic questions found in 3:1-5. In 3:6-25 Paul has discussed the theological basis for issues such as the purpose of the law, the

---

[57] Gk. πρὸ τοῦ δὲ ἐλθεῖν τὴν πίστιν
[58] Gk. ἐλθούσης δὲ τῆς πίστεως
[59] A great deal of research has gone into Paul's use of the term παιδαγωγός. See bibliography containing list of articles in Kruse, *Paul,* 94. Whatever the nuances of this term, for our purposes it is sufficient to note the temporary nature of the law: ἐλθούσης δὲ τῆς πίστεως οὐκέτι ὑπὸ παιδαγωγόν ἐσμεν "now that faith has come we are no longer under the supervision of the law" (3:25).
[60] Here in Galatians Paul doesn't specifically tell us *why* the arrival of Christ put an end to the supervisionary role of the law. Rather, he just tells his readers this is the case. It is doubtless difficult to pull all of Paul's statements about the law into one coherent whole, and this exercise is made more difficult by the tendency of many to dichotomize Paul's statements: Either the law is said to be fully valid today, or fully abrogated. Carson comments, "But may we not argue that in one sense the law *is* 'out of date and irrelevant' (consider what Paul says about circumcision, Rom. 2.28-29; 1 Cor. 7.19; Gal. 5.6!), yet in another sense, though it is along the salvation-historical plane 'out of date', it has continuing functions, not only to provide warnings (I Cor. 10.11), but *typoi* (I Cor. 10.6,11) and witness (Rom. 3.21), enabling us thereby to discover the law's valid continuity in that to which it points." D. A. Carson, "Pauline Inconsistency: Reflections on I Corinthians 9.19-23 and Galatians 2.11-14," *Churchman* 100 (1986): 36. Carson also adds, "Whatever other functions the law has in Paul's theology—and it has many—one important element is its anticipation of the fuller revelation found in Christ himself. The law is not so much abrogated as *fulfilled* along a salvation-historical axis" (italics mine). Ibid., 37.

relationship of Christ and his death to the law, the relationship of the Gentiles to the promise, the relationship of Abraham to Christ. But now it is time for Paul to bring these truths to bear on the situation at hand, specifically his confrontation with Peter in Antioch (2:11-14).

First, Paul clearly desires to emphasize that *all* Galatian believers are sons of God because they are in Christ; there is no distinction, all are sons of God by nature of their relationship to Christ. Second, for the first time the concept of being *in Christ* appears. This reality is expressed many ways in 3:26-29: "in Christ Jesus"[61] (3:26, 28), "baptized into Christ,"[62] (3:27) "clothed . . . with Christ,"[63] (3:27), and "belong to Christ"[64] (3:29). Just as Jews were *in* Abraham (3:8), believers, both Jew and Gentile, are *in* Christ. Third, the tie between Abraham (including the promise made to him) and Christ is made explicit (3:29): Those in Christ are heirs of Abraham and heirs of the promise.

## THE ROLE OF GALATIANS 3:28 IN PAUL'S ARGUMENT

Galatians 3:28, if removed from its context in Galatians 3–4, contains no specific indicators of its salvation-historical importance. Within the flow of Paul's argument, however, it is clear that with the arrival of Christ (3:23, 25) and the coming of the Spirit (3:14; 4:6) there has been a redefining of the people of God.[65] Peter's decision to refrain from eating with Gentiles is blameworthy on many accounts, but it is certainly wrong on the grounds that Gentiles and Jews are now one in Christ—and any behavior that implies that Gentiles are not fully God's people is to be condemned.[66]

> The promise to Abraham has come. Whatever redemptive-historical purposes were served by protecting and distinguishing Israel from the

---

[61] Gk. ἐν Χριστῷ Ἰησοῦ
[62] Gk. εἰς Χριστὸν ἐβαπτίσθητε
[63] Gk. Χριστὸν ἐνεδύσασθε
[64] Gk. ὑμεῖς Χριστοῦ
[65] I borrow this phrase from Charles B. Cousar, *A Theology of the Cross: The Death of Jesus in the Pauline Letters* (Minneapolis: Fortress, 1990), 111.
[66] When Peter opted not to eat with Gentiles, he returned to a "'minority' period of the history of the Jewish race (4.1-7)." Carson, "Pauline Inconsistency," 20. By doing this, Peter demonstrated that he obviously did not understand the ramifications of Christ's death. Furthermore, many would interpret his behavior, in itself harmless, as teaching that law observance was a requirement for "staying in" and, by association, for "getting in" as well. As Carson notes, "Peter had given the impression that the best Christians must be circumcised and come under the law of Moses, and that threatened the gospel that Peter and Paul shared." Ibid., 34.

Gentiles, the time has now come when the ascended Christ has poured out his Spirit on the Gentiles, winning them to faith in the God of Abraham. The Gentiles are no longer enemies of Abraham's descendants; they *too* are Abraham's descendants. Consequently, to exclude the Gentiles is an eschatological, christological, and ecclesiastical error of great magnitude.[67]

The full inclusion of the Gentiles into the people of God is an important eschatological event, predicted from the beginning in the promise first made to Abraham (Gen. 12:3; 18:18). Paul has had the Gentiles in mind throughout the book. At the beginning he establishes that the gospel he preaches is not his message but God's (1:11), and this authoritative gospel clearly includes the Gentiles (cf. 3:8). He reminds the Galatians that his divine calling and mission was *to* the Gentiles (1:15-16; 2:2, 7-8, 9). Then he links Christ's death to the inclusion of the Gentiles into the blessings promised to Abraham (3:14).

By tailoring his account as he does, he asserts that the inclusion of the Gentiles was not a dimension of the gospel he invented or developed later in his preaching ministry; rather it was an essential feature constitutive of the gospel as first revealed to him. The non-acceptance of the Gentiles, then, represents for Paul a faulty interpretation of the one, true gospel.[68]

Galatians 3:28 describes the inclusion of the Gentiles, an event signifying that a new period of redemptive history has dawned. To miss the significance of this is to miss what God has done.

It is important to understand the flow of Galatians 3–4 in order to rightly interpret Galatians 3:28. If one does not comprehend the significance of the salvation-historical story line in these two chapters, specifically the redefining of the people of God in the new era, it is not possible to understand what Paul intended when he wrote, "There is neither Jew nor Greek, slave nor free, male nor female, for you are all one in Christ Jesus."

---

[67] T. David Gordon, "The Problem at Galatia," *Interpretation* 41 (1987): 38-39.
[68] Normand Bonneau, "The Curse of the Law in Gal. 3:10-14," *Novum Testamentum* 39, no. 1 (1997): 64.

*Excursus: The "New Perspective on Paul" and Galatians 3:28*

There is a new paradigm in Pauline studies, often referred to as the "new perspective on Paul." While this "new perspective" is far from mono-lithic, several tendencies are observable among most adherents. The pur-pose of this excursus is to mention briefly how this "new perspective" might bear on the interpretation of Galatians 3:28. It is beyond the scope of this summary to delineate all the major proponents or tenets of this school of thought.

Fundamentally, those who advocate a "new perspective" on Paul agree with a salvation-historical reading of Galatians 3–4, sharing much in common with what is presented in this chapter. The inclusion of Gentiles into the people of God is a critical theme in Galatians, they argue. And, correspondingly, Galatians 3:28 should be interpreted in this light. In this sense, my position perhaps finds greater affinity with proponents of the "new perspective" than with traditional interpreters. In the past, a works/faith dichotomy has flavored interpretations of Galatians, with justification by faith being viewed as the dominant motif in Galatians and other themes being subsumed in its shadow. Moo com-ments, "Certainly some more traditional approaches have been guilty of underestimating the role of historical and corporate factors in Paul's polemic and of too readily assuming a stereotypic 'legalistic' view of Paul's opponents."[69]

The new perspective on Paul denies that Galatians is primarily about justification or works-righteousness, and that Judaism was a works-oriented religion. Instead, it argues that Galatians is about sal-vation-history and Paul's attempt to deal with the inclusion of the Gentiles. The law must be done away with because it "fosters Jewish exclusiveness"[70] and prohibits Gentiles from being part of the people of God. Paul is "down" on the "works of the law" simply because they are Jewish identity markers, not because they are works in contrast to faith. As David Gordon comments, "The polemic is not in the first place sote-riological (that is, faith or works as an instrument of justification) but eschatological (whether God has fulfilled the promises to Abraham by means of the Christ-event) and, by consequence, ecclesiological (whether

---

[69] Moo, "Paul and the Law in the Last Ten Years," 298.
[70] Ibid.

the believing Gentiles are in fact full members of the covenant community)."[71] So, beginning with the primacy of salvation-history in Paul's thought, proponents of the "new perspective" often end up redefining, or even devaluing, the doctrine of justification.

While I embrace the priority of the salvation-historical flow in Galatians 3–4, in no way do I affirm any redefining or devaluing of justification by faith. We will not explore the details of this discussion;[72] it is sufficient for our purposes to note that one's interpretation of Galatians 3:28 is not necessarily affected by one's prior commitment to the "new perspective" on Paul.

---

[71] Gordon, "The Problem at Galatia," 40.

[72] Many scholars have argued against the position, or at least the exclusive claims, of the "new perspective." See for example Westerholm, Schreiner, Kruse, Moo, and Mark Seifrid, *Justification by Faith: The Origin and Development of a Central Pauline Theme* (Leiden, Netherlands: E. J. Brill, 1992).

# THE IMMEDIATE CONTEXT:
# GALATIANS 3:26-29

Having examined the importance of salvation-history to Paul's argument in Galatians 3–4, we must now exegete 3:26-29 with the purpose of understanding 3:28 in its immediate context. There is no lack of writing on Galatians 3:28; surprisingly, however, very few of these works explore the contextual, lexical, and syntactical issues important to understanding it. The task of this chapter is to examine the critical exegetical issues found in Galatians 3:26-29, paying special attention to those issues most pertinent to an accurate interpretation of 3:28.

Galatians 3:26-29 functions as a hinge, tying Paul's discussion on the promise and the relationship of the law to the promise (3:15-25) with the new sonship status of those who are now, with the arrival of Christ, full heirs of the promise (4:1-7). Structurally, Galatians 3:26-29 is fairly straightforward, though some see the traditions that lie behind these verses as complex.[1]

## THE STRUCTURE OF GALATIANS 3:26-29

A structural diagram of Galatians 3:26-29 reveals that this section is framed by two clauses, 26a and 29: "You are all sons of God[2] . . . then you are Abraham's seed, and heirs according to the promise."[3] These clauses

---

[1] Longenecker speculates a "sayings" statement (v. 26), a confessional portion (vv. 27-28), and a concluding statement (v. 29). Richard Longenecker, *Galatians,* Word Biblical Commentary (Dallas, Tex.: Word, 1990), 150-151.

[2] Gk. Πάντες γὰρ υἱοὶ θεοῦ ἐστε

[3] Gk. ἄρα τοῦ Ἀβραὰμ σπέρμα ἐστέ, κατ᾽ ἐπαγγελίαν κληρονόμοι

summarize this section and succinctly highlight its function as a pivot between the promises made to Abraham (3:15-25) and those who are now in Christ (4:1-7). A simple structural diagram of 3:26-29 looks like this:

26 You are all sons of God
            through faith in Christ Jesus,
27        for all of you who were baptized into Christ
            have clothed yourselves with Christ
28            There is neither Jew nor Greek,
           slave nor free,
           male nor female,
       for you are all one
           in Christ Jesus.
29       If you belong to Christ,
    then you are Abraham's seed,
       and heirs according to the promise.[4]

It is noteworthy that the often-cited verse 28 is, in context, not an isolated saying but rather an integral part of a larger argument that is framed by the two clauses in verses 26 and 29. The importance of this observation will be elaborated upon below.

## GALATIANS 3:26

3:26-29 is intricately tied to what precedes (3:23-25) and what follows (4:1-7), yet these verses are also a unit in their own right, as evidenced by the following:

- in 3:26-29 there is a shift in pronouns to the second person; the preceding section (3:23-25) is in the first person and the following section (4:1-7) is in the third person;

---

[4] 26 Πάντες γὰρ υἱοὶ θεοῦ ἐστε
     διὰ τῆς πίστεως ἐν Χριστῷ Ἰησοῦ·
27 ὅσοι γὰρ εἰς Χριστὸν ἐβαπτίσθητε,
     Χριστὸν ἐνεδύσασθε.
28    οὐκ ἔνι Ἰουδαῖος οὐδὲ Ἕλλην,
     οὐκ ἔνι δοῦλος οὐδὲ ἐλεύθερος,
     οὐκ ἔνι ἄρσεν καὶ θῆλυ·
     πάντες γὰρ ὑμεῖς εἷς ἐστε
         ἐν Χριστῷ Ἰησοῦ.
29   εἰ δὲ ὑμεῖς Χριστοῦ,
    ἄρα τοῦ Ἀβραὰμ σπέρμα ἐστέ,
    κατ᾽ ἐπαγγελίαν κληρονόμοι

- as shown above, two phrases frame this section: "you are all sons . . . then you are Abraham's seed" (vv. 26, 29);

- the structure of 3:26-29 reveals a self-contained argument;[5]

- 4:1 begins with "What I am saying is . . . ,"[6] which transitions to an elaboration of the implications of verse 29.

### *"[For] you are all sons of God . . ."*

There is a conjunction in the Greek[7] not translated by the NIV that emphasizes the connection between this unit (3:26-29) and the previous unit (3:23-25); the reason that the Galatians are "no longer under the supervision of the law" (v. 25) is because ("for") they are now "sons of God through faith in Christ Jesus" (v. 26). Longenecker comments, "The postpositive γάρ [the Greek conjunction left out by the NIV] here has both explanatory and continuative functions, and so is probably to be translated "for, you see . . ."[8] As we have noted, although this section is joined with what precedes it, it is set off by a change in pronouns, from the first person plural "we" to the second person plural "you."

Paul often switches pronouns, and Galatians is an example *par excellence*. For example, note how he switches from the first person comment, "I do not set aside the grace of God" (2:21) to the second person exhortation, "You foolish Galatians!" (3:1). Then he moves from the third person Old Testament quote, "The man who does these things will live by them" (3:12) to the first person plural, "[Christ] redeemed us in order that the blessing given to Abraham might come to the Gentiles" (3:14). Some argue that Paul uses first person plurals in Galatians to refer to the Jews (cf. 2:15) and then switches to second person plural when he addresses the primarily Gentile Galatian church (compare, e.g., 3:23-25 to 3:26-29; 4:3-5 to 4:6ff.; and 4:26 to 4:28).[9] Yet it is difficult to account for every pronoun change using this schema,

---

[5] This is clearer in the Greek, as the NIV has smoothed over some of the Greek prepositions. The Greek structure has γὰρ . . . γὰρ . . . γὰρ . . . ἄρα. Literally in English it would be *"for* you are all sons, *for* you are all baptized into Christ, *for* you are all one in Christ . . . *therefore* you are Abraham's seed, heirs of the promise."

[6] Gk. Λέγω δέ

[7] Gk. γάρ

[8] Longenecker, *Galatians,* 151.

[9] See T. L. Donaldson, "The 'Curse of the Law' and the Inclusion of the Gentiles: Galatians 3.13-14," *New Testament Studies* 32 (1986): 94-112; and D. W. B. Robinson, "The Distinction Between Jewish and Gentile Believers in Galatians," *Australian Biblical Review* 13 (1965): 29-48.

for some switches in Galatians appear to be ambiguous,[10] and Paul is
fond of pronoun switches, often seemingly without warrant.[11] Note that
the terminology in 3:23-35 ("we were held prisoners by the law . . . we
are no longer under the supervision of the law") fits a Jewish referent
best, though nothing in 3:23-25 absolutely precludes Gentiles. What
does seem clear, however, is that the pronoun switch minimally serves
to focus Paul's teaching directly upon the Galatians: "*You* are all sons
of God . . ." (cf. 3:1; italics mine).[12] It is also important to note the inclusive "all" here in verse 26, which will appear again in verse 28. We will
explore later the importance of this universal term.

Although twentieth-century American Christians likely find nothing
shocking about the statement, "you are all sons of God through faith in
Christ Jesus," this was probably not the case with the Galatian readers.
First, the *universal nature* of the declaration would have been startling;
Paul declares that *all* Galatians, Jews and Gentiles alike, are sons.[13]
Though the Old Testament foretold of the Gentiles being included in the
promises to Abraham (Gen. 12:1-3; 18:18; Isa. 49:5-6), the statement
that Gentiles are now heirs and sons would have been noteworthy.

---

Donaldson and Robinson, citing particularly 3:13-14, 3:23-29, and 4:3-7, argue that the first person plurals in Galatians refer to the Jews, and the second person plurals refer to the Gentiles.
Following this distinction, Robinson argues that those "whom Christ redeemed through his death
from the curse of the law were *Jews*." Robinson, "Jewish and Gentile Believers," 34. Donaldson,
while affirming the salvation-historical primacy of the Jews, wisely backs away from stating that
Christ's death was for the Jews alone. Instead he states that God used the law to create a "representative sample in which the human plight is concentrated and clarified." Donaldson, "The
'Curse of the Law'," 106. Thus, the Jews have a unique, fundamental role, but "the redemption
of Israel is at the same time and on the same terms the redemption of the Gentiles." Ibid.

[10] For example, the "we" in 3:14 seems to include both Jews and Gentiles, as does the "we" in
4:5.

[11] C. E. B. Cranfield, "Changes of Person and Number in Paul's Epistles," in *Paul and Paulinism:
Essays in Honour of C. K. Barrett*, eds. M. D. Hooker and S. G. Wilson (London: SPCK, 1982),
280-289.

[12] Peter O'Brien makes this point regarding Ephesians 2, where some have similarly argued that
the "we" pronouns have Jewish referents and the "you" pronouns refer to Gentiles. O'Brien, however, citing A. T. Lincoln and others, postulates that the pronoun changes most likely are made
to focus on the Galatian readers. Thus, the "we" terms would refer to believers in general and the
"you" terms would highlight the Galatian readers, who would include both Gentiles and Jews.
This proposal seems to fit the Galatian evidence as well. Peter T. O'Brien, "Divine Analysis and
Comprehensive Solution: Some Priorities from Ephesians 2," *The Reformed Theological Review*
53:3 (September–December 1994): 132.

[13] The term *sons* here in Galatians 3–4 surely includes all individuals, male and female. There is
a strong universal emphasis in this passage. I will use the term *sons* instead of *children* throughout the book for three reasons: 1) the NIV uses this terminology; 2) the Greek term υἱοί is usually
translated "sons." In light of the universal language throughout the passage, there is little chance
that anyone could be confused and perhaps feel left out by the use of *sons* to represent all believers; 3) switching from *sons* to *children* could perhaps hide the connection Paul makes in 4:4-5,
4:6, and 4:7 between God's Son and our inheritance/status as "sons."

Second, the very *nature* of the declaration would have been surprising; the Galatian believers are now actually sons of God.[14] While the Old Testament acknowledged God as Father (Deut. 32:6; Isa. 63:16; 64:8), and the people of Israel were infrequently called his "sons" (Ex. 4:22-23), sonship is not a prevalent concept in the Old Testament.[15] The New Testament term for adoption[16] is not found in the Greek version of the Old Testament (Septuagint)[17] and the New Testament sonship available through faith in Christ is qualitatively different than sonship under the old covenant. Paul makes this clear in what follows (Gal. 4:1-7), where he contrasts "children . . . in slavery under the basic principles of the world" with children who have "the full rights of sons." No one, for example, in the Old Testament would have considered addressing God as "*Abba*, Father" (Gal. 4:6). In summary, the inclusion of the Gentiles and the blessing of the "full rights" of sonship (4:5) both signify the advent of the "fulness of the time" (4:4, NASB).

### ". . . through faith in Christ Jesus,"

The final clause in verse 26, "through faith in Christ Jesus,"[18] consists of two phrases. "Through faith"[19] designates the means by which sonship is available. The term *faith*[20] occurs twenty-two times in Galatians in a variety of constructions, but primarily with a preposition (fifteen times), as here.[21] In the Greek there is an article before the word *faith*,

---

[14] Gk. υἱοὶ θεοῦ

[15] For example, there are more references to God as "Father" in a single NT book, such as Matthew, or John, than can be found in the entire OT. See, however, Willem A. VanGemeren, "Abba in the Old Testament?" *Journal of the Evangelical Theological Society* 31 (1988): 385-398, who argues that "The OT cautiously attributes Fatherhood to Yahweh." Ibid., 392.

[16] Gk. υἱοθεσία

[17] Ferguson rightly points out, however, that in certain passages "the Old Testament pictures the salvation of God's people in language which is tantamount to adoption." Sinclair B. Ferguson, "The Reformed Doctrine of Sonship," in *Pulpit and People: Essays in Honour of William Still on His 75th Birthday,* eds. Nigel M. de S. Cameron and Sinclair B. Ferguson (Edinburgh: Rutherford, 1986), 85. Also see James M. Scott, *Adoption as Sons of God: An Exegetical Investigation into the Background of HUIOTHESIA in the Pauline Corpus,* Wissenschaftliche Untersuchungen zum Neuen Testament 2.48 (Tübingen: J. C. B. Mohr, 1992), who likewise argues for an OT background to the concept of adoption presented in Galatians 3–4.

[18] Gk. διὰ τῆς πίστεως ἐν Χριστῷ Ἰησοῦ

[19] Gk. διὰ τῆς πίστεως

[20] Gk. πίστις

[21] It occurs three times with διά, eleven times with ἐκ, and once with ἐν. When it is not used with a preposition, five times πίστις is used in the nominative or accusative as a substantive (1:23; 3:23[2x]; 5:6, 22) and twice in the genitive (3:25, 6:10). The expression διὰ τῆς πίστεως is virtually indistinguishable from ἐκ πίστεως. Murray Harris notes: i) both expressions may mean either "through faith" or "by faith"; ii) in places Paul seems to use these expressions interchange-

which likely points to the personal nature of the Galatians' faith: "through faith, that is, *your* faith."[22] It is not uncommon to find Paul using this expression, *through faith,* either with or without the article.[23]

The second phrase, "in Christ Jesus,"[24] is a well-used Pauline expression and a key concept not only for this passage but for the entire book of Galatians as well. Sonship is available only in God's Son, *in Christ.* Sinclair Ferguson comments, "It is because he [Christ] has entered our family that we enter the family of God (Heb. 2:5-18)."[25]

How is the first phrase, "through faith," related to the second phrase, "in Christ Jesus"? One option is to make "Christ Jesus" the object of the faith; hence, sonship comes through faith *in Christ.* Supporting this view is the parallel with Abraham in Genesis 15:6; Abraham believed *in Yahweh,*[26] and it was credited to him as righteousness.[27]

While there is no doubt that the New Testament teaches that one believes *in Christ,* there is other evidence that indicates the primary function of the phrase "in Christ Jesus" is not to designate the object of faith. Two observations are significant. First, this construction is somewhat rare in Paul; there are only four examples where he follows "faith" with this particular preposition[28] (cf. Eph. 1:15; Col. 1:4; 1 Tim. 3:13; 2 Tim. 3:15).[29] More importantly, as Burton points out, Paul always uses a different form (the genitive case) in Galatians to denote the *object* of faith.[30]

---

ably (e.g., Gal. 2:16, Rom. 3:25-26); iii) elsewhere Paul can use either expression to denote the cause of justification or the cause of sanctification; and, iv) stylistic variation, including switching these two phrases, is common for Paul (e.g., Rom. 3:24). Both of these prepositional phrases have an instrumental force, "through (or by) faith." Murray J. Harris, "Prepositions and Theology in the Greek New Testament," *The New International Dictionary of New Testament Theology,* 3 vols., ed. Colin Brown (Grand Rapids, Mich.: Zondervan, 1971), 3:1189-1190. For examples with ἐκ see Rom. 5:1; 9:30; for examples with διά see Rom. 3:22; Eph. 2:8.

[22] Longenecker, *Galatians,* 152; E. de Witt Burton, *A Critical and Exegetical Commentary on the Epistle to the Galatians,* International Critical Commentary Series (Edinburgh: T. & T. Clark, 1921), 203, italics mine.

[23] Eight times, in addition to Galatians 3:26, Paul uses this expression with the article: Rom. 3:25, 30, 31; Gal. 3:14; Eph. 3:12, 17; Col. 2:12; and 1 Thess. 3:17. Nine times Paul uses it without the article: Rom. 3:22, 27; 4:13; 2 Cor. 5:7; Gal. 2:16; Eph. 2:8; Phil. 3:9; and 2 Tim. 3:15.

[24] Gk. ἐν Χριστῷ Ἰησοῦ

[25] Ferguson, "The Reformed Doctrine of Sonship," 87.

[26] Heb. בִּיהוָה

[27] Longenecker, *Galatians,* 153.

[28] πίστις followed by ἐν

[29] Murray J. Harris, "Prepositions and Theology in the Greek New Testament," *The New International Dictionary of New Testament Theology,* 3 vols., ed. Colin Brown (Grand Rapids, Mich.: Zondervan, 1971), 3:1212; Burton, *Galatians,* 202.

[30] Burton, ibid.

What, then, is the appropriate sense of this phrase? Galatians 3:14 provides help, as it is the only other location in Galatians where the phrase "in Christ Jesus" is found in proximity to "through faith."[31] In 3:14 the blessings of Abraham come *in Christ* and are received *through faith*. The force, then, of 3:26 would be something like, "You are all sons of God, through faith, *by being in Christ.*" Being a son of God is tied to being *in Christ.* This corporate view of being "in Christ" is found in the following verses (vv. 27, 28), providing further confirmation that this is the proper interpretation of the expression the NIV renders "through faith in Christ Jesus." We will give further attention to the expression "in Christ" when we encounter it in verse 28.

Sonship, then, is tied to being in Christ, and it is now available through faith. This is the primary emphasis of the verse. "Christians are not primarily sons of Abraham because of their 'faith' (vv. 6-9); they are primarily sons of God (v. 26) because they have been incorporated in Christ."[32] The idea of Christ as the object of our faith is important, and certainly true, but as Burton comments, it is a "secondary and suggested thought" in verse 26.[33]

Verse 26 is an important transition. Paul turns from his commentary on the progress of salvation-history to address the Galatians: "*You* are all sons of God through faith in Christ" (italics mine). He insists that:

- *All* Galatians are in the same position—there is no distinction when it comes to being a member of God's household.

- The Galatians are now *sons of God,* an incredible blessing from God.

- The basis for this blessing is because they are *in Christ.* Just as the promise given to Abraham was for those "in him," now, in the fullness of time, the privilege of sonship is tied to being in God's Son.

---

[31] Gk. διὰ τῆς πίστεως
[32] J. C. Beker, *Paul the Apostle: The Triumph of God in Life and Thought* (Philadelphia: Fortress, 1980), 50-51.
[33] Burton, *Galatians*, 203.

- The means by which it is possible to be in Christ is through *faith*.

Two of the concepts introduced here—the universal nature of God's blessing, coming to all Galatians, and the incorporation of God's people in Christ—introduce key concepts for the interpretation of Galatians 3:28.

## GALATIANS 3:27

Verse 26 introduced the concept of sonship that, in Christ, is available through faith. Now, in verse 27, Paul utilizes two word pictures, baptism and being clothed with Christ, to elaborate further on the concept of being "in Christ" (v. 26). We could spend a great deal of time on Paul's theology of baptism, or the implications of being clothed with Christ, but because of our focus on 3:28, we will look at these issues only briefly.

### *"for all of you who were baptized into Christ . . ."*

The pronoun "all of you who"[34] (v. 27) refers back to "sons of God" (v. 26); those who are in Christ are sons of God (v. 26), and these are those who have been baptized into Christ and clothed with Christ (v. 27). The close link between verse 26 and verse 27 shows that, in Paul's thought, faith is closely tied to baptism. Longenecker comments that these two concepts, while being distinct in Paul's thought, are "always related, though never thought of as identical or supplements to one another."[35] Baptism is so closely aligned with salvation in the New Testament that often baptism can, by metonymy, stand for the whole conversion experience.[36]

So the expression "baptized into Christ" refers to the believer's "rite of initiation into Christ, that is, into union with Christ."[37] Paul simply

---

[34] Gk. ὅσοι

[35] Longenecker, *Galatians*, 156.

[36] A metonymy is a figure of speech where the part stands for the whole. A modern-day equivalent might be the slang phrase, "I walked the aisle when I was twelve." The speaker uses the phrase "walked the aisle" to stand for the entire conversion experience, not implying that the actual act of walking the aisle either produced the conversion or was the same thing as the conversion. Dr. Carson provided this helpful analogy.

[37] Ronald Y. K. Fung, *The Epistle to the Galatians*, The New International Commentary on the New Testament Series (Grand Rapids, Mich.: Eerdmans, 1988), 172.

points to the baptism of the Galatians as a reminder that they are indeed in Christ and thus are sons of God

**"... *have clothed yourselves with Christ.*"**

Paul uses a second image to describe those in Christ: They have "put on Christ" (KJV, RSV). Some commentators, such as Beasley-Murray, see the first phrase "baptized into Christ," as the cause and the second phrase, "clothed with Christ," as the effect: "We should not regard baptism to Christ . . . as being identical with putting on Christ; rather the former act has the latter state as its effect."[38] J. D. G. Dunn counters, "In other words, to be baptized into Christ is the *same thing* as putting on Christ."[39] There is little profit in laboring to adjudicate this minor discrepancy: Beasley-Murray affirms that all who have been baptized have put on Christ, which is, bottom line, quite similar to Dunn. Either way, believers are "clothed with Christ."

What is the meaning of the metaphor "clothed with Christ"? Paul often uses this verb[40] to construct metaphors, usually with an impersonal object.[41] His use of this type of metaphor has Old Testament precedent, as Beasley-Murray notes: "The imagery of stripping off clothes and putting on fresh ones to indicate a transformation of character is frequent in the OT (e.g., Isa. 52:1; 61:10; Zech. 1:1-5)."[42] For example, Isaiah 61:10 states, "I delight greatly in the LORD . . . for he has clothed me with garments of salvation"; and in Psalm 35:26 David writes, "May all who exalt themselves over me be clothed with shame and disgrace."

But here this verb is used with a personal object, Christ. Burton comments, "Used with an impersonal object, it [this verb] means 'to acquire,' 'to make a part of one's character or possessions' (1 Thess. 5:8; 1 Cor. 15:53, 54 ; Rom. 13:12; Col. 3:12); with a personal object it signifies 'to take on the character or standing' of the person referred to, 'to

---

[38] G. R. Beasley-Murray, *Baptism in the New Testament* (Grand Rapids, Mich.: Eerdmans, 1962), 129.

[39] James D. G. Dunn, *Baptism in the Spirit* (London: SCM, 1977), 112, italics mine.

[40] Gk. ἐνδύω

[41] "Put on the armor of light" (Rom. 13:12); "put on the Lord Jesus Christ" (Rom. 13:14, NASB); "put on the imperishable" and "put on immortality" (1 Cor. 15:53, NASB); "put on the new self" (Eph. 4:24); "put on the full armor of God" (Eph. 6:11); "put on the breastplate of righteousness" (Eph. 6:14, NASB); "put on the new self" (Col. 3:10); "put on a heart of compassion" (Col. 3:12, NASB); "put on the breastplate of faith" (1 Thess. 5:8, NASB).

[42] G. R. Beasley-Murray, "Baptism," *Dictionary of Paul and His Letters*, eds. Gerald F. Hawthorne and Ralph P. Martin (Downers Grove, Ill.: InterVarsity, 1993), 62.

become,' or 'to become as.'"[43] Burton also adds that this idiom "conveyed no suggestion of putting on a mask, but referred *to an act in which one entered into actual relations.*"[44] Thus the metaphor, in this context, while certainly including a change in status or character, expresses the reality that "by faith the Christian shares the sonship of the Christ in whom he lives."[45]

In summary, verse 27 clarifies verse 26. Paul reminds the Galatians, by an allusion to their baptism, of their conversion experience; and then, by use of a clothing metaphor, he points to their changed character and union with Christ. All the Galatian believers have been baptized into Christ and have clothed themselves with him. While there are different nuances to these two expressions, for our purposes it is sufficient to note that these phrases are true of *all* Galatian believers and that they simply elucidate Paul's central affirmation that the Galatians are *in Christ*. It is the reality of being "in Christ" that makes it possible to be sons of God and heirs of the promise. And now, in verse 28, Paul turns to describe the "oneness" that exists in Christ.

## GALATIANS 3:28

Verse 28 can now be unpacked in light of its context. The verse consists of three couplets and a final clause, which provides the reason for the negation of the three couplets. The couplets are parallel except for a change from one conjunction[46] in the first two couplets to another[47] in the third. While the syntax of verse 28 is simple enough, its meaning and significance is ardently contested.

Prior to examining the verse, we must consider briefly the commonly asserted proposal that Galatians 3:28 contains a pre-Pauline baptismal formula. Many scholars, including Longenecker[48] and Betz,[49] think this is the case. They note that a possible parallel in 1 Corinthians 12:13 mentions baptism, and Colossians 3:11, another possible paral-

---

[43] Burton, *Galatians*, 204.
[44] Ibid., italics mine.
[45] Ibid.
[46] Gk. οὐδέ. This negative conjunction is usually translated "nor."
[47] Gk. καί. This conjunction is usually translated "and."
[48] Longenecker, *Galatians*, 153-156.
[49] H. D. Betz, *A Commentary on Paul's Epistle to the Galatians*, Hermenia (Philadelphia: Fortress, 1979), 181-185.

lel, appears in a context that alludes to baptism. In addition, it is argued that since the final two couplets (slave/free, male/female) are foreign to Paul's argument in Galatians to this point, the presence of the couplets is evidence that Paul is citing an existing creed.[50]

The possibility of these couplets being an early baptismal formula is certainly an option, yet substantiating this thesis is difficult. Dunn notes:

> That such a liturgy fitted his argument so neatly is by no means impossible, though the existence of such elaborate liturgies at this early stage is questionable (see my *Unity* 141-7); and when the key evidence is from the Pauline letters themselves, it becomes methodologically difficult to distinguish more widespread patterns from characteristic Pauline themes and forms.[51]

There are also differences between the so-called parallels. The 1 Corinthians 12:13 parallel makes no reference to the male/female couplet when, given the content of the letter (especially chapters 7, 11, and 14), one would expect this couplet to be mentioned. The Colossians 3:11 parallel likewise fails to mention the male/female couplet and includes a couplet (circumcised/uncircumcised) and two other groups of people (Barbarian, Scythian) left out of both Galatians 3:28 and 1 Corinthians 12:13. If one argues that the existence of the two unexpected couplets in Galatians 3:28 is positive evidence for an early creed, what weight should be placed on the fact that one of the couplets (male/female) doesn't occur anywhere else, even when one might expect it? Furthermore, the conjunctions and syntax used in each of the three supposed parallel passages is far from consistent.[52] Dunn notes, "The for-

---

[50] Many scholars have noted that parts of these three couplets show up in Jewish and Greco-Roman sources. Because of this some are persuaded that a connection might exist between Galatians 3:28 and these sources; others remain unconvinced. Klyne Snodgrass mentions several possible parallels. In the end he views most of them as likely irrelevant to an interpretation of Galatians 3:28. One possible parallel can't be ruled out, according to Snodgrass, but there is no way of knowing for sure. Klyne Snodgrass, "Galatians 3:28: Conundrum or Solution?" *Women, Authority, and the Bible* (Downers Grove, Ill.: InterVarsity, 1986), 168-171.

[51] James D. G. Dunn, *The Epistle to the Galatians,* Black's New Testament Commentaries (Peabody, Mass.: Hendrickson, 1993), 201.

[52] Note the change in conjunctions and syntax: Gal. 3:28: Ἰουδαῖος οὐδὲ Ἕλλην, δοῦλος οὐδὲ ἐλεύθερος, ἄρσεν καὶ θῆλυ ("Jew nor Greek, slave nor free, male and female"); Col. 3:11: Ἕλλην καὶ Ἰουδαῖος, περιτομὴ καὶ ἀκροβυστία, βάρβαρος, Σκύθης, δοῦλος, ἐλεύθερος ("Greek and Jew, circumcised and uncircumcised, barbarian, Scythian, slave, free"); 1 Cor. 12:13: εἴτε Ἰουδαῖοι εἴτε Ἕλληνες εἴτε δοῦλοι εἴτε ἐλεύθεροι ("whether Jews or Greeks or slaves or free").

mulations are sufficiently varied to show that it was not a fixed formula so much as a cherished theme."[53] The idea of these couplets being an early baptismal creed is intriguing, but speculative. As Betz adds, with a note of caution, "One may therefore *venture the suggestion* that Paul has lifted Galatians 3:26-28, in part or as a whole, from a pre-Pauline liturgical context."[54] In any case, variations between the so-called parallels should warn against placing too much interpretive weight on the existence of an early baptismal formula. Maybe such a saying existed, maybe it didn't. In either case the interpretation of this verse should not be affected by the hypothetical existence of an early creed.[55]

Now to the verse itself. The structure of Galatians 3:28 is as follows: "not this . . . *because* of this."[56] Each couplet is negated in light of the reason given in 28d: "for you are all one in Christ Jesus." We will first examine these couplets individually, but because their meaning hinges, to a large degree, on the intent of the final clause ("for you are all one in Christ Jesus"), we will need to withhold final conclusions regarding the significance of these couplets until we have considered all of verse 28. Because of the nature of our study, we will give more attention to the exegetical and lexical issues in the final couplet than in the first two.

*"There is neither Jew nor Greek, . . ."*

Each of the three couplets in Galatians 3:28 begins with the same Greek expression, [57] translated in the NIV as either "there is neither" or "nor." Lexicons generally agree that the phrase is equivalent to "there is no

---

[53] James D. G. Dunn, *The Epistles to the Colossians and to Philemon: A Commentary on the Greek Text*, NIGTC (Grand Rapids, Mich.: Eerdmans, 1996), 223.

[54] Betz, *Galatians*, 184, italics mine.

[55] Some who propose that Galatians 3:28 is an early baptismal creed see great interpretive significance in this "fact." Scholer states, "Second, it is most likely that the triple pairing found in Galatians 3:28 is an intentional use of a long-standing and culturally diverse tradition and of a somewhat fixed formulaic device. Thus, Paul's theological affirmation in Galatians 3:28 is at the same time a strong statement with traditional and cultural overtones, which identifies the text as horizontal as well as vertical." David M. Scholer, "Galatians 3:28 and the Ministry of Women in the Church," in *Theology, News and Notes* (Pasadena, Calif.: Fuller Theological Seminary, June 1998), 19-22. Since this is an early creed, Scholer argues, it has horizontal significance. I am suggesting, however, that it is mere speculation to label Galatians 3:28 an early creed; and, correspondingly, it is illegitimate and unwise to place interpretative significance on such a "hypothetical maybe."

[56] Ben Witherington III, "Rite and Rights for Women," *New Testament Studies* 27 (1981): 596, italics mine.

[57] Gk. οὐκ ἔνι

. . .",[58] but disagreement exists concerning the lexical background of the phrase.[59] I did a search using the Thesaurus Linguae Graecae (TLG) data base[60] for all occurrences of this expression[61] from the second century B.C. through the first century A.D. Apart from the three uses in Galatians 3:28, my search uncovered sixteen other occurrences of this phrase; ten of these occurrences were with an infinitive.[62] In the uses with the infinitive the expression had the sense, "it is not possible." For example, Dio Chrysostomus, *Orationes* 31.51.2: "It is *impossible* for anything thus administered to be annulled"; and *Orationes* 75.10.3: "A city *cannot* be saved if the law has been destroyed." Also Appian, *Roman History* 4.4.28: "It is *not permitted* me to escape"; and *Roman History* 5.5.42.19: "It is *not in my power* to speak otherwise."

The other six examples were more like Galatians 3:28, occurring without the infinitive. In these cases the meaning was "there is not": Arrian, *Indica* 26.7.4: ". . . for *there is no* grass in the place"; Plutarch, *Adversus Colotem* 1114.E.2: ". . . and a man's beliefs, that *lack* all true persuasion"; *Sib Or.* 3.358: "As a slave you will be wed *without* decorum"; James 1:17: ". . . with whom *there is no* variation, or shifting shadow" (NASB); 1 Corinthians 6:5: "Is it possible *there is nobody*

---

[58] BAGD, 265; MM, 215; and LSJ, 567 see the expression as equivalent to ἐστί, hence best translated "there is no. . . ."

[59] There is disagreement over the lexical background of ἔνι. BAGD, MM, BDF and others view ἔνι as a shortened form of ἔνεστιν, from ἔνειμι. Others, such as Burton, see it as a lengthened form of the preposition ἐν. Burton, *Galatians*, 207. While the issue may never be ultimately resolved, Meyer's insight is important: "Very frequently ἔνι and ἐν are used together, and yet there is no ἐστί added, whereby the ἔνι shows that it stands independently as a compound word = ἔνεστι or ἔνεισι." Heinrich Meyer, *Epistle to the Galatians*, trans. G. H. Venables (New York: Funk & Wagnalls, 1884), 157. These occurrences where ἔνι is used with ἐν provide good evidence that ἔνι comes from ἔνεστιν, and that this term is not simply a lengthened form of ἐν. A New Testament example of ἔνι used with ἐν can be found in 1 Corinthians 6:5: οὕτως οὐκ ἔνι ἐν ὑμῖν οὐδεὶς σοφός: "There is nobody among you wise." As Burton notes, however, "the word [ἔνι] never quite loses the force derived from ἐν, as a preposition of place." Burton, *Galatians*, 20. This is evident in Galatians 3:28, as οὐκ ἔνι, used here with "in Christ" language, appears to retain the force of ἐν; there is no Jew/Greek *in* Christ. At times ἔνι can have a slightly different nuance. BAGD notes that ἔνεστιν, from ἔνειμι, can also mean "it is possible." BAGD, 264. The negative expression οὐκ ἔνι would then mean "it is not possible."

[60] Thesaurus Linguae Graecae is a data base of ancient Greek texts between Homer and A.D. 600. By last count it contains 65,000,000 occurrences of Greek words penned by 3,165 authors. The data base is exhaustive, containing "virtually all authors represented by text, whether in independent editions or in quoted form."

[61] Gk. οὐκ ἔνι

[62] Appianus, *Libyca* 415.8, *Roman History* 4.4.28, 5.5.42.19; Dio Chrysostomus, *Orationes* 31.25.9, 31.51.2, 31.102.6, 75.10.3; Dionysius Halicarnassensis, *de Demosthensis dictione* 15.20, 22.30, 43.55. All original source translations are from the Loeb Classical Series unless noted otherwise.

among you wise enough to judge?"; Colossians 3:11: "Here *there is no* Jew or Greek."

This expression, then, is best translated "there is not," but when used with an infinitive it usually has the sense of "it is not possible." This is confirmed by the lexical evidence and by our examination of every use of the expression in the three centuries around the New Testament. The six uses without an infinitive are clearly better rendered "there is not," rather than "it is not possible." Thus, the expression in the three couplets is best captured by "there is not" (in Christ) Jew or Greek, slave or free, male or female.[63]

This first couplet, "Jew nor Greek,"[64] clearly fits within the flow of the argument Paul has been developing from the start of chapter 3, though one might have expected Jew/Gentile[65] instead of Jew/Greek. J. Wanke comments, however, that though the basic meaning for the term Paul chose[66] is "Greek," "in many passages the meaning 'Gentile' resonates [for this term] . . . especially where 'Jews and Hellenes' represents the totality of mankind divided according to a salvation-historically relevant distinction (Acts 19:10; 20:21; Rom. 1:16; 2:9f; 3:9; 10:12; 1 Cor. 1:24, etc.)."[67] For example, the couplet found in Galatians 3:28a is used by Paul in Romans 2:9 to refer to every human being: "There will be trouble and distress for every human being who does evil, first for the Jew, then for the Gentile."[68] Windisch notes, "There can thus be no doubt that Paul includes the Ἕλληνες [Greeks] among the ἔθνη [Gentiles] and often uses the words interchangeably. Nevertheless, they are not quite identical. This is proved by the use of Ἕλληνες [Greeks] as a national term when the parallel word does not occur."[69] Here in

---

[63] Most modern translations have captured this well: "There is neither . . ." (NIV, NASB, NKJV, RSV, KJV). The NRSV translates "There is no longer," implying the end of Jew/Greek, slave/free, male/female distinctions. Perhaps this idea was added by the translators in light of the salvation-historical context, but "no longer" is not a viable translation for οὐκ ἔνι. Likewise, *The Jerusalem Bible* imports too much into the word when it translates οὐκ ἔνι, "there are no more distinctions." The Weymouth translation, "there cannot be," appears to have given οὐκ ἔνι the meaning "it is not possible," versus the more appropriate "there is not."

[64] Gk. Ἰουδαῖος οὐδὲ Ἕλλην

[65] Gk. Ἰουδαῖος/ ἔθνη

[66] Gk. Ἕλλην

[67] J. Wanke, " Ἕλλην," *EDNT*, 1:436. See also Acts 14:1; Rom. 1:16; 2:10; 3:9; 10:12; Gal. 2:3.

[68] Note that the NIV chose to translate Ἕλλην in Romans 2:9 as "Gentile."

[69] H. Windisch, "Ἕλλην," *TDNT*, 2:516. The "Ἕλληνες are . . . one great half of the race to whom the Gospel is to be taken . . . that part of the race which is distinguished from the Jews by language, descent and culture." Ibid., 513.

Galatians 3:28, used in a salvation-historical situation in conjunction with "Jews," Ἕλληνες ["Greeks"] is interchangeable with ἔθνη [Gentiles] (cf. Gal. 2:2-3). The couplet Jew/Greek is significant from a salvation-historical perspective[70] and together, as a pair, they represent all of humanity.

After we examine the other two couplets, we will return to examine further the meaning of this couplet.

*". . . slave nor free, . . ."*

The slave/free couplet is somewhat unexpected, as Paul has made no mention of either group in his letter thus far. Because Paul extensively develops the slave metaphor in 4:1ff., some have posited that the introduction of this couplet here is simply to set up forthcoming portions of the letter. This is plausible, yet because no such explanation is easily identifiable for the third couplet, male/female, it is likely that this slave/free couplet is introduced, at least in part, for another reason.

It is difficult for any twentieth-century American to read the word "slave" without immediately reflecting upon the institution of slavery as it was practiced in America in the eighteenth and nineteenth centuries. Slavery in New Testament times was different in many crucial respects. There were slaves from different races, slaves who volitionally chose to sell themselves into slavery for economic reasons, and slaves from all walks of life, "from laborers to philosophers, from farmers to physicians."[71] While a detailed description of New Testament slavery is not necessary for our present inquiry, it is important to note that the slave/free distinction was the primary *legal* distinction for all people: "Gaius, the Roman jurist whose *Institutes* are the most complete Roman law book that has come down to us from near the time of Paul, states that the basic distinction in the law of persons is that all men are either free or slaves."[72] Spicq notes that, prior to being used for slaves, the term δοῦλος [slave] "was an adjective meaning 'unfree,' as opposed to *eleutheros* [free], and this dichotomy remained basic in the first cen-

---

[70] Both here in Galatians and all throughout Scripture the gospel/promise is described as coming first to the Jews, then to the Gentiles.

[71] Ceslas Spicq, *Theological Lexicon of the New Testament*, trans. and ed. James D. Ernest (Peabody, Mass.: Hendrickson, 1994), 1:383.

[72] Francis Lyall, *Slaves, Citizens, Sons: Legal Metaphors in the Epistles* (Grand Rapids, Mich.: Zondervan, 1984), 35.

tury: *eite douloi, eite eleutheroi* [either slave or free]."[73] Thus, one of
the most basic distinctions in life was that a person was viewed as either
slave or free.

Paul's inclusion of the slave/free couplet, then, is like the Jew/Greek
couplet. From a Jewish perspective, all the world can be divided into two
parts, Jew and Gentile; likewise, from a legal perspective, all the world
is either slave or free. These are two of the most fundamental ways of
viewing the world in New Testament times. A third most basic way of
dividing the world appears in the third couplet: male and female.

### ". . . *male nor female*, . . ."

This couplet is joined by a different conjunction than the first two.[74]
Some commentators, including Richard Longenecker[75] and F. F. Bruce,[76]
see little change in meaning in this switch. Virtually all translations of
the Bible (except the NRSV) concur, as the last couplet in these versions
is translated in the same way as the first two: "There is neither Jew nor
Greek, slave nor free, male *nor* female." Other scholars, such as Klyne
Snodgrass,[77] view the change in conjunctions as significant, as a delib-
erate move by Paul to refer to Genesis 1:27 in the Septuagint. When the
Septuagint refers to the creation of man and woman in Genesis 1:27, it
uses the exact same construction: "Male *and* female he created them."[78]
I will try to show that there is truth in both of these positions; there is
persuasive evidence that Galatians 3:28 refers to Genesis 1:27, yet the
parallelism between the three couplets, each contrasting opposites, provides good reason to translate each of them in the same manner.

The words Paul chose for "male and female"[79] are rather rare in the
New Testament,[80] and are not the terms one might have expected. These
two terms are used to express "emphatic sexual differentiation."[81] In
Romans 1:26-27 Paul uses the two terms in discussing male and female

---

[73] Spicq, *Lexicon*, 380.
[74] καί rather than οὐδέ
[75] Longenecker, *Galatians*, 157.
[76] F. F. Bruce, *The Epistle to the Galatians*, New International Greek Testament Commentary
(Grand Rapids, Mich.: Eerdmans, 1982), 189.
[77] Snodgrass, "Galatians 3:28," 171.
[78] Gk. ἄρσεν καὶ θῆλυ ἐποίησεν αὐτούς
[79] Gk. ἄρσεν καὶ θῆλυ
[80] ἄρσεν in Matt. 19:4; Mark 10:6; Luke 2:23; Rom. 1:27 (3x); Gal. 3:28; Rev. 12:5, 13. θῆλυ
in Matt. 19:4; Mark 10:6; Rom. 1:26, 27; Gal. 3:28.
[81] A. Oerke, "ἀνήρ," *TDNT*, 1:362.

sexual functions: "Even their women[82] exchanged natural relations for unnatural ones. In the same way the men[83] also abandoned natural relations with women[84] and were inflamed with lust for one another. Men committed indecent acts with other men.[85]" Jesus, citing Genesis 1:27, uses these terms in his teaching on the inappropriateness of divorce in Matthew 19:4: "'Haven't you read,' he replied, 'that at the beginning the Creator "made them male and female."'"[86] Luke, citing the Old Testament law found in Exodus 13, writes, "As it is written in the Law of the Lord, 'Every firstborn male[87] is to be consecrated to the Lord'" (Luke 2:23). In the Septuagint the term Paul uses for "male" in Galatians 3:28 often refers to a male sacrificial animal: "He is to offer a male without defect" (Lev. 1:3), or to circumcision: "Every male in the city was circumcised" (Gen. 34:24). An interesting passage in Genesis 17:23 highlights the sexual nature of this term: "Abraham brought *every male of the men*[88] of his household to be circumcised."[89]

These two particular Greek words for "male and female"[90] are used often in Genesis 6–7 with reference to the animals in the ark; but when the phrase is used with reference to humans, it virtually always refers to Genesis 1:27. This is true in the New Testament (Matt. 19:4 and Mark 10:6) and in the Septuagint (Gen. 5:2). I did a TLG search for every extrabiblical occurrence of this phrase from the second century B.C. through the first century A.D. and found that all four uses of this expression refer back to Genesis 1:27.[91] In light of the uniform use of this phrase (in the Septuagint, New Testament, and three centuries around the New Testament), the switch in conjunctions, and the use of the somewhat rare nouns, it is best to conclude that Paul deliberately referenced Genesis 1:27 in this couplet.[92]

---

[82] Gk. θήλειαι
[83] Gk. ἄρσενες
[84] Gk. θηλείας
[85] Gk. ἄρσενες ἐν ἄρσεσιν
[86] Gk. ἄρσεν καὶ θῆλυ
[87] Gk. ἄρσεν
[88] Gk. πᾶν ἄρσεν τῶν ἀνδρῶν
[89] Literal translation mine. One wonders about the self-esteem of any "man" who was left out by Abraham!
[90] Gk. ἄρσεν καὶ θῆλυ
[91] Philo, *Here.* 164.5; Clement of Rome, *Epistle to 1 Corinthians* 33.5.3; *Epistle to 2 Corinthians* 14.2.3; *Homiliae* 3.54.2.4.
[92] It is, however, possible to argue *against* a tie to Gen. 1:27 by noting how Paul varies his choice of conjunctions in the two parallels, Col. 3:11 and 1 Cor. 12:13. Paul joins the couplet ῞Ελλην

Paul's apparent negation of Genesis 1:27 (*"neither . . .* male [and] female"—Gal. 3:28) has prompted a few scholars, such as Betz, to propose that Paul is advocating androgyny: Now, in Christ, there is neither male nor female; that is, salvation brings about the "metaphysical removal of *biological* sex distinctions."[93] This seems far-fetched, as by Betz's own admission Paul makes no reference to an androgynous Christ or an androgynous Christian. Nevertheless, Betz proposes:

> The *possibility*, however, that the Christ-Anthropos myth lies behind Galatians 3:28 cannot be excluded. . . . *If the assumption is made* that behind Galatians 3:28c lies a doctrine of an androgynous Christ-redeemer, the implication would be that the dissolution of the sexual distinctions is coupled with a christology in which Christ figures as the androgynous Anthropos. Being "one in Christ Jesus" (Galatians 3:28d) would then be a form of "imitation of Christ" and would follow from the inclusion of the Christian into the "body of Christ." Since Christ is androgynous, his "body" would be also, and so would the Christians who are members of that body.
>
> Thus the *hypothesis* can be proposed that this doctrine lies behind Galatians 3:28, *although definite proof is impossible for lack of sources.*[94]

Despite Betz's hypothesis, Galatians 3:28c does not teach androgyny. Paul elsewhere affirms sexual distinctions (Rom. 1; 1 Cor. 7; 1 Tim. 2; Titus 2; etc.), not the creation of a single sex. Furthermore, the Scriptures clearly teach that God created mankind "male and female" prior to the fall, and this was good (Gen. 1:27, 31). In *every* instance where a biblical author cites Genesis 1–2, describing God's pre-fall creation, the reference is positive;[95] there is no reason to believe that Galatians 3:28 is the first exception. Finally, as Witherington notes, Colossians 3:11, a close parallel of Galatians 3:28, teaches that "putting

---

and Ἰουδαῖος with οὐδέ in Gal. 3:28 and then, in the exact same construction, uses καί in Col. 3:11. Maybe, then, his switch in Gal. 3:28 from οὐδέ in the first two couplets to καί in the last couplet is only stylistic and is not meant to refer to Gen. 1:27. (In 1 Cor. 12:13 the choice of conjunctions is different altogether from both Gal. 3:28 and Col. 3:11.) As argued above, however, Paul's choice of the rare words (ἄρσεν and θῆλυ), coupled with the switch to καί, make it more likely that Paul *did* intend to refer to Gen 1:27.
[93] Betz, *Galatians*, 196.
[94] Ibid., 199, italics mine. Betz is right: Any hypothesis can be proposed, although it would be preferable that such a hypothesis would have some sort of evidence behind it.
[95] For a complete list of quotations and allusions to Genesis 1–2, see appendix in NA 27, 770ff.

on Christ" is in fact "being renewed in the image of the Creator."[96] The expression "there is no male and female" may be difficult, but it certainly cannot mean the abolition of males and females.

It is highly likely, then, that the third couplet of Galatians 3:28 ("neither . . . male nor female") refers to Genesis 1:27. The precise meaning of the negation in this couplet, as well as the negation in the other two, will be considered after we examine the final clause of verse 28.

### ". . . for you are all one . . ."

The final clause of verse 28, "for you all are one in Christ Jesus," is the crux of the verse; whatever Paul meant by the preceding three couplets he bases on this truth. The word *for*[97] introduces the grounds for what has gone before: There is no Jew or Greek, slave or free, male and female *for* "you are all one in Christ Jesus." It is interesting that this concept of oneness is also apparent in the so-called parallels in 1 Corinthians 12:13 and Colossians 3:11.[98]

Paul delineates six different groups of people who are said to "be one" in Christ: Jews, Greeks, slaves, free, males, and females. All humanity, regardless of religious/ethnic heritage, legal status, or sexual identity, are said to be one in Christ. Questions, nevertheless, remain about this expression. What does it mean for a diverse plurality to "be one"? If a plurality is "one," what does this imply about the *relationship between* the parts? If a plurality is "one," what does this imply about the *function* of the parts? For example, if Jews and Greeks are one in Christ, does this change how Jews and Greeks relate to one another? If so, how? While it is not possible to form complete answers to all these questions given the brevity of this phrase, it is important to examine thoroughly the meaning and implications of "you are all one in Christ" in order to come to a proper understanding of Galatians 3:28.

Two observations are pertinent prior to examining the concept of oneness. First, Paul has repeatedly emphasized the universal nature of being in Christ: *All* the Galatian believers are sons of God, *all* have been

---

[96] Witherington, "Rite and Rights," 598. Being "renewed in the image of the Creator" affirms differences between male and female, as Genesis 1:27 states: "So God created man in his own image, . . . male and female he created them."

[97] Gk. γάρ

[98] 1 Cor. 12:13, "one body"; Col. 3:15, "since as one body you were called to peace."

baptized into and clothed with Christ, *all* are now one in Christ Jesus. Second, the present tense verb[99]—"you *are* all one in Christ"—highlights the ongoing, vivid reality of being one in Christ; all the Galatians are presently one in Christ.

What does it mean for a plurality to be one? We will answer this question first by examining the lexical possibilities for the word *one*. Then we will examine other uses of this same expression, where a plurality of objects or people are said to "be one."[100] What other plurality of objects or people are said to "be one"? What can we learn about Galatians 3:28 from other uses of the same expression?

## LEXICAL POSSIBILITIES FOR "ONE"[101]

BAGD lists the following lexical options for the Greek word translated "one" in Galatians 3:28.[102] It will be convenient to present them in outline form:

1. Literal Uses
   A. In contrast to more than one
      i. as an adjective: "one baptism" (Eph. 4:5)
      ii. as a noun with a partitive genitive: "one of these" (Matt. 6:29)
   B. In contrast to the parts of which a whole is made: "We, who are many, form one body" (Rom. 12:5)
   C. With a negative following: "Not one of them will fall"[103] (Matt. 10:29)
2. Emphatic Uses
   A. One and the same: "one and the same loaf" (1 Cor. 10:17)
   B. Single, only one: "he had an only son" (Mark 12:6)
   C. Alone: "who can forgive sins but God alone?" (Mark 2:7)
3. Indefinite Uses
   A. Someone, anyone: "one of the prophets" (Matt. 16:14)
   B. As an indefinite article: "a scribe" (Matt. 8:19)

---

[99] Gk. ἐστε
[100] plural form of ἐμί with a nominative form of εἷς, μία, ἕν.
[101] Gk. εἷς
[102] BAGD is the standard Greek lexicon for the NT. BAGD, 230-232.
[103] The examples given by BAGD are Matt. 5:18; 10:29; Mark 8:14; Luke 11:46; 12:6. In each of these verses, as noted by BAGD, the Greek has the negative *following* the form of "one." But in each case the NIV translation places the negative before the form of "one," e.g. Matt. 10:29, "*Not one* of them will fall"; and Luke 12:6, "Are not five sparrows sold for two pennies? Yet *not one* of them is forgotten by God."

C. Used with τὶς [an indefinite pronoun]: "a certain young man" (Mark 14:51, NRSV)
4. Perhaps as a Hebraism: "on the first day of the week" (1 Cor. 16:2)
5. Different special combinations

The term *one* in Galatians 3:28, then, can have many different uses in the New Testament. BAGD lists Galatians 3:28 as an example of 1.B., where "one" emphasizes the whole in contrast to the parts. Paul is highlighting the whole ("you all are *one* in Christ Jesus") in contrast to the parts (Jew/Greek, slave/free, male/female).

Stauffer, in a major article in *TDNT*, notes the variety of ways this word is used in the New Testament: "Only rarely is εἷς ["one"] used as a digit in the NT (e.g., 2 Pt 3:8). It usually means 'single,' 'once-for-all,' 'unique' or 'only,' or 'unitary,' 'unanimous,' or 'one of two or many,' only one."[104] Here in Galatians 3:28, according to Stauffer, Paul is emphasizing the unity of the people of God. Stauffer notes that just as the destiny of the human race was decided in Adam, so, in Christ, the "destiny of the new humanity is determined."[105]

So there are many lexical possibilities for "one,"[106] but both Stauffer and BAGD state that this term, as used in Galatians 3:28, denotes a unity, the whole in contrast to the parts. It is important at this point simply to note that the lexical possibilities for this word do not include "equal."[107] Correspondingly, the *lexical* options for "you are one" do not include "you are equal." We will consider the idea of equality in the next chapter.

One further question remains regarding this term *one:* One what? While it is clear that Paul uses *one*, a masculine singular form, to denote a unified whole, the text doesn't tell us what the word *one* modifies. Elsewhere in the New Testament the feminine form of *one*[108] is used with the feminine noun *flesh:*[109]—"one flesh" (Mark 10:8). Likewise, the

---

[104] E. Stauffer, "εἷς," *TDNT*, 2:434.
[105] Ibid., 439.
[106] Gk. εἷς
[107] I am indebted to Ann Coble's thesis for this observation. Ann Coble, "The Lexical Horizon of 'One in Christ': The Use of Galatians 3:28 in the Progressive-Historical Debate over Women's Ordination," Th.M. thesis, Covenant Theological Seminary, 1995.
[108] Gk. μία
[109] Gk. σάρξ

neuter form for *one*[110] is used with the neuter noun *body:*[111]—"one body" (Rom. 12:5). But here the masculine form of *one* stands alone, without a noun. The New Testament has other examples of this: "Now he who plants and he who waters are one"[112] (1 Cor. 3:8, NASB); or "I and the Father are one"[113] (John 10:30). F. F. Bruce argues that the apostle's thought is much like Romans 12:5: "So we, who are many, are one body in Christ" (NASB).[114] But if Paul wanted to say "one body," one wonders why he chose the masculine form instead of the neuter.[115] While we might never know with certainty to what the term *one* is linked, the sense of Galatians 3:28 is clear enough: Jew/Greek, slave/free, male/female are united in a "new oneness" in Christ, in which all believers, of all types, share.[116]

## PARALLEL EXPRESSIONS

In an effort to understand the expression "you [plural] are one"[117] I did a search for similar uses of this phrase in Greek, where a plural form of this verb[118] was coupled with a form of "one."[119] I searched all known Greek literature written in the three centuries from the second century B.C. through the first century A.D., using TLG. I ran forty-five searches, looking for parallel expressions.[120] What other things, or people, were

---

[110] Gk. ἕν
[111] Gk. σῶμα
[112] Gk. neuter ἕν
[113] Gk. neuter ἕν
[114] Bruce, *Galatians*, 190.
[115] C. K. Barrett suggests that, if one must supply a noun, the masculine εἷς must be tied to the masculine υἱός (son). "The noun we must put with the numeral 'one' is 'son.' Paul remembers, and is now about to return to, his (to our minds) forced observation regarding the 'one seed' of Abraham. . . . *You* are the one seed; Paul declares this explicitly in 3.29. If you belong to Christ (a variant way of saying 'If you are in Christ'), then you are Abraham's seed (σπέρμα, singular) heirs (κληρονόμοι, plural) in terms of promise." C. K. Barrett, *Freedom and Obligation: A Study of the Epistle to the Galatians* (Philadelphia: Westminster, 1985), 38. I am hesitant to say that all believers are one Son, simply because the Scripture does not use this type of language to describe our incorporation in Christ; rather, they (believers) are all one seed. The many are sons of God and heirs of the promise by virtue of being in the one Son who is the one heir of the promise.
[116] Longenecker, *Galatians*, 158.
[117] Gk. ὑμεῖς εἷς ἐστε
[118] Gk. εἰμί
[119] Gk. εἷς, μία, or ἕν
[120] The search was for uses of a plural form of εἰμί coupled with a nominative form of εἷς, μία, or ἕν. I looked for only nominative forms of εἷς, μία, and ἕν in light of their use with a copulative verb. TLG searched for plural forms of εἰμί within six words of a nominative form εἷς, μία, or ἕν. These were the plural forms searched: present indicatives ἐσμέν, ἐστέ, εἰσίν, εἰσί; future indicatives ἐσόμεθα, ἔσεσθε, ἔσονται; imperfect indicatives ἦμεν, ἤμεθα, ἦτε, ἦσαν; and subjunctives ὦμεν, ἦτε, ὦσιν, ὦσι. I sought matches within six words for any of these forms with either of the three nominatives for "one." For complete results of this search, see the appendix.

said to "be one"? I found sixteen similar expressions in these 300 years, some of which are quite helpful toward understanding Paul's use of this phrase in Galatians 3:28:

Occurrences of ἐσμέν with ἕν ("We are one.")
1. John 10:30
   ἐγὼ καὶ ὁ πατὴρ ἕν ἐσμεν
   "I and the Father are one."
2. Romans 12:5
   οὕτως οἱ πολλοὶ ἕν σῶμά ἐσμεν ἐν Χριστῷ
   "... so we, who are many, are one body in Christ." (NASB)
3. 1 Corinthians 10:17
   ὅτι εἷς ἄρτος, ἕν σῶμα οἱ πολλοί ἐσμεν
   "Since there is one bread, we who are many are one body."
   (NASB)
4. Ignatius, *Epistulae interpolatae et epistulae suppositiciae*
   11.4.2.5[121]
   ἵνα, ὡς ἐγὼ καὶ σὺ ἕν ἐσμεν, καὶ αὐτοὶ ἐν ἡμῖν ἕν ὦσιν
   "so that as you and I are one, also they may be one in us."

Occurrences of ἐστέ with εἷς ("You are one.")
5. Galatians 3:28
   πάντες γὰρ ὑμεῖς εἷς ἐστε ἐν Χριστῷ Ἰησοῦ
   "... for you are all one in Christ Jesus."
6. Dio Chrysostom, *Orationes* 41.10.7
   καὶ σχεδὸν εἷς ἐστε δῆμος καὶ μία πόλις ἐν οὐ πολλῷ
   διαστήματι
   "You are almost one community, one city only slightly
   divided."

Occurrences of εἰσίν with εἷς ("They are one.")
7. Philo, *De Mutatione Nominum* 200.2
   οἱ δὲ πρὸς ἄμυναν εὐτρεπεῖς τῶν οὕτως βεβήλων καὶ
   ἀκαθάρτων τρόπων δύο μέν εἰσιν ἀριθμῷ, Συμεὼν καὶ
   Λευί, γνώμῃ δὲ εἷς
   "... and the champions who stand ready to repel such pro-
   fane and impure ways of thinking are two in number,
   Simeon and Levi, but they are one in will."

---

[121] This portion of Ignatius' Epistle to the Ephesians is missing from most manuscripts, including the volume *The Apostolic Fathers* in the Loeb Classical Library. This text is from the TLG database, which gives its source as *Patres Apostolici*, eds. F. X. Funk and F. Diekamp, vol. 2, 3rd ed. (Tübingen: Laupp, 1913), 234-258. Translation is mine.

Occurrences of εἰσί with εἶς ("They are one.")

8. Philo, *Legum Allergoriarum* 3.105.4

ὁρᾷς ὅτι κακῶν *εἰσι* θησαυροι · καὶ ὁ μὲν τῶν ἀγαθῶν *εἶς*—ἐπεὶ γὰρ ὁ θεὸς *εἶς*, καὶ ἀγαθῶν θησαυρὸς «*εἶς*»

"You see that there are treasuries of evil things. And the treasury of good things is one, for since God is One, there is likewise one treasury of good things."

Occurrences of εἰσίν with μία ("They are one.")

9. Matthew 19:6

ὥστε οὐκέτι *εἰσὶν* δύο ἀλλὰ σὰρξ *μία*

"So they are no longer two, but one."

10. Mark 10:8

ὥστε οὐκέτι *εἰσὶν* δύο ἀλλὰ *μία* σάρξ

"So they are no longer two, but one."

Occurrences of εἰσίν with ἕν ("They are one.")

11. 1 Corinthians 3:8

ὁ φυτεύων δὲ καὶ ὁ ποτίζων *ἕν εἰσιν*

"Now he who plants and he who waters are one" (NASB).

12. 1 John 5:8

τὸ πνεῦμα καὶ τὸ ὕδωρ καὶ τὸ αἷμα, καὶ οἱ τρεῖς εἰς τὸ *ἕν εἰσιν*

". . . the Spirit, the water and the blood; and the three are in agreement."

Occurrences of ὦσιν with ἕν ("They may be one.")

13. John 17:11

ἵνα *ὦσιν ἕν* καθὼς ἡμεῖς

". . . so that they may be one as we are one."

14. John 17:21

ἵνα πάντες *ἕν ὦσιν*

". . . that all of them may be one."

15. John 17:22

ἵνα *ὦσιν ἕν*

". . . that they may be one."

16. John 17:22

καθὼς ἡμεῖς *ἕν*

". . . as we are one."

17. John 17:23

ἵνα *ὦσιν* τετελειωμένοι εἰς *ἕν*

". . . that they may be perfected in unity" (NASB).

The sixteen occurrences other than Galatians 3:28 fall into several categories. It is helpful to group these as follows:

| *Different Elements* | *One _____?* |
|---|---|
| Jesus/Father (John 10:30; 17:11, 21, 22 [2x], 23; *Epistulae* 11.4.2.5) | one nature? |
| Husband/wife (Matt. 19:6; Mark 10:8) | one flesh |
| Different believers (Rom. 12:5; 1 Cor. 10:17) | one body |
| Planter/waterer (1 Cor. 3:8) | one purpose? |
| Spirit, water, blood (1 John 5:8) | one witness |
| 2 cities | one community |
| 2 people, Simeon and Levi (*De Mutatione Nominum* 200.2) | one will |
| Many good things (*Legum Allergoriarum* 3.105.4) | one treasury/ one God |

We can draw several observations from all the occurrences of a plural form of εἰμί coupled with *one*. These will be quite helpful in understanding Galatians 3:28:

i) Diverse people and objects are said to "be one." For example, the one who plants is different from the one who waters; each has a different role and reward, though both are said to be one (1 Cor. 3:8). Members of the body of Christ have different gifts and functions, but together they are said to form one body (Rom. 12:5). Two cities, though separated geographically, are said to be "almost one community." The expression "we/you/they are one" is used precisely *because* it serves to unify *different* people and objects. This is always the case. There are no exceptions where two identical, or very similar, objects are said to be "one."

ii) While the expression "we/you/they are one" unifies *different* people and objects, the separate elements, however, do have something in common. In nearly half of the occurrences this is clearly stated by the author: e.g., one flesh, one will, one community. In the remaining cases, although the referent is not clearly stated, it is usually easily discernible. For example, when the one who plants and the one who waters are said to be one, no referent is given, but *one purpose* can be assumed.

Likewise, when the Father and the Son are said to be one, the referent, though not given, can be assumed to be *one essence* or *nature*. (Yet here, too, they are different persons with different roles.)

iii) The expression "we/you/they are one" doesn't provide specific details about the individual elements that are united, except that the individuals are "one" in some respect. The reader is informed as to what the different elements have *in common*, not as to how each element compares to, or relates with, the other. For example, Philo notes that Simeon and Levi are one in will and purpose, but beyond that it is not possible to know, for example, if Levi is brighter than Simeon, if Simeon resents Levi, or if Simeon is Levi's boss. All one knows is that the two men are united in will and purpose. Likewise, a husband and a wife become one flesh, but this expression, in itself, does not inform the reader as to how husbands and wives should relate to each other. It simply informs the reader that two individuals are now one flesh. Doubtless there are ramifications to becoming one flesh, but the expression doesn't provide the details; instead, it emphasizes that the husband and wife are one flesh.

In summary, the expression "you are all one" does not provide specifics regarding the relationship between the parts. Rather, the expression simply states that diverse parts share something in common; they are united in some respect, in contrast to their diversity. Lexically the word *one*[122] can be used many ways, but not to denote equality. In Galatians 3:28 this word is used to express unity in distinction to a plurality: Jews/Greeks, slaves/free, males/females, by virtue of each sharing in one Christ, are one.

### ". . . *in Christ Jesus.*"
In Galatians 3:26-29 Paul uses several expressions to denote the reality of being intimately associated with Christ: "in Christ Jesus" (vv. 26, 28),[123] "into Christ" (with the verb *to baptize*, v. 27)[124] "with Christ" (with the verb *to clothe*, v. 27),[125] and "belong to Christ" (v. 29).[126] It

---

[122] Gk. εἷς
[123] Gk. ἐν Χριστῷ Ἰησοῦ
[124] Gk. εἰς Χριστόν
[125] Gk. Χριστόν with ἐνδύω
[126] Gk. the genitive Χριστοῦ

has long been recognized that the concept of being "in Christ" is central to Pauline theology, as he uses these expressions more than 160 times.[127] The variation in expressions found in Galatians 3:26-29 is not unlike the rest of the Pauline corpus; Paul prefers "in Christ" (twenty-six times),[128] "in Christ Jesus" (forty-two times),[129] and "in the Lord" (forty-seven times),[130] but many other alternative phrases (such as "into Christ," 3:27) are used as well.[131] Most scholars agree on two general conclusions concerning the Pauline evidence: i) the variation of expressions points to a "field of meaning" rather than a single technical sense;[132] and ii) Paul's variation is not solely stylistic, but patterns can be observed that shed light on the precise nuance of a particular usage. While a complete survey of Paul's uses of the "in Christ" expression is beyond the scope of this work, the "in Christ" theme is important for Galatians 3–4, and for Galatians 3:26-29 in particular.

Galatians 3:6-29 develops an argument using Abraham. In 3:8 Paul reminds his readers of the promise to Abraham: All the nations of the earth will be blessed through Abraham ("through you"[133]); in 3:28-29 this promise given to Abraham is tied to being in Christ: "If you belong to Christ, then you are Abraham's seed, and heirs according to the promise" (v. 29). So, it is being "in Christ" (v. 28) that is key to being Abraham's seed and receiving the promised inheritance.

Paul uses the phrase "in Christ" in a variety of ways. At least three particular truths communicated by this expression are important for our passage:

i) Paul often uses "in Christ" terminology to signify the outworking of God's plan of redemption in salvation-history. For example, "In him we have redemption" (Eph. 1:7). "Everything that God has planned

---

[127] Deissmann's study in 1892 on Paul's use of ἐν Χριστῷ is generally considered the "starting point" for current proposals on the meaning of this phrase. By his count Paul uses the term 164 times. Walter Bartling, "The New Creation in Christ," *Concordia Theological Monthly* 21, no. 6 (June 1950): 401.
[128] Gk. ἐν Χριστῷ
[129] Gk. ἐν Χριστῷ Ἰησοῦ
[130] Gk. ἐν [τῷ] Κυρίῳ
[131] See the helpful breakdown of variations of this phrase in N. T. Wright, *The Climax of the Covenant* (Minneapolis: Fortress, 1991), 44-45.
[132] M. A. Seifrid, "In Christ," in *The Dictionary of Paul and His Letters*, eds. Gerald F. Hawthorne and Ralph P. Martin (Downers Grove, Ill.: InterVarsity, 1993), 433.
[133] Gk. ἐν σοὶ

for the salvation of fallen man, everything that He has done in history for man's redemption, He has planned and executed *in Christ Jesus.*"[134] In Galatians 3–4 God's plan of redemption is clearly identified with "in Christ" language; the blessing given to Abraham now comes to the Gentiles so that both Jews and Gentiles, by faith, might receive the promise of the Spirit (Gal. 3:14). This is all done in/through Christ Jesus; "to be *in Christ* is to be taken up into the sphere of God's redemptive activity."[135]

ii) Being "in Christ" also means being incorporated into Christ.[136] This is shown by Paul's argument here in Galatians 3–4; those who inherit the promise given to Abraham are those who are incorporated into Abraham; they are called his seed (v. 29). Since Christ is the Seed of Abraham, those who belong to Christ share in Abraham's blessing. Being "in Christ," then, is being incorporated with him so that one becomes a child of God (v. 26) and a recipient of the promise simply because of one's union with him.

iii) Being "in Christ" is not simply an individual issue; being "in Christ" means being placed into a new community or body: "The new creation is the community which Christ has established and which has its life *in Him.* . . . [Becoming a new creation] is an intensely personal matter. That is never denied. But it is also and always a communal matter. . . . To belong to the community is to be *in Christ;* to be *in Christ* is

---

[134] Bartling, "New Creation," 402, italics his.

[135] Ibid., 403. For other examples of "in Christ" used to "relate the effects of God's redemptive activity to believers," see Rom. 8:1; 1 Cor. 1:30; 2 Cor. 5:21.

[136] Scholars have debated the nature of this union or incorporation. For our purposes, it is only necessary to recognize that being "in Christ" means being intimately identified with him. He is our representative, and we share in him. This identification/union is complex but nevertheless real. In Romans 6 Paul uses the similar phrase "*with* Christ" to describe a believer's union with Christ. If being "in Christ" was some sort of symbolic relationship, "dying" and "rising" with Christ, as presented in Romans 6, would not be in the realm of possibility. Paul uses language which reveals that this union/incorporation was quite substantial. For example, at the end of Galatians he writes, "May I never boast except in the cross of our Lord Jesus Christ, *through which the world has been crucified to me, and I to the world*" (6:14, italics mine). Bartling suggests, "The central Pauline concept of *being in Christ* is an extension of the type of thinking which can view an individual as the representative and inclusive personality of an entire race of men, with whom he is related by ties of blood or through necessities arising out of the order of creation." Bartling, "New Creation," 412. This seems correct, but, as already noted, understanding the nuances of the union resulting from being "in Christ" is not necessary for this project. It is enough to affirm the reality of being incorporated with him.

to belong to the community."[137] Here in Galatians 3:28 the communal nature of being "in Christ" could not be more evident: Jews/Greeks, slaves/free, males/females are all one *in Christ*. Being in Christ has consequences for how one relates to other members of the community.

J. C. Beker uses a completely different, and insightful, approach in describing Paul's use of "in Christ":

> The motif [the incorporation motif—being in Christ] . . . has several components in Paul: (1) the one for all; (2) the one in all [and all in one]; (3) the once for all. The "once for all" expresses the eschatological-historical event of Jesus Christ (cf. Rom. 5:15-19; 6:10) that marks the end of the old age and the inauguration of the new age. The "one for all" describes the death of Christ as the act of God's grace for his people, who henceforth participate in him ("the one in all" and "all in one"; cf. Rom. 5:12-19, 1 Cor. 15:22).[138]

Here in Galatians 3, all three aspects are clearly seen: the "one for all" is seen by Christ being our representative Seed; the "one in all" and "all in one" is seen in that Jew/Greek, etc., are incorporated in Christ;[139] and the "once for all" is highlighted by the forthright salvation-historical argument. Christ is the one for all, and all are in him, the One; as a result, all are one.

In summary, the negation of the three couplets is based on the truth that, "You are all one in Christ Jesus." Murray Harris paraphrases it this way: "You are all one *by being in Christ Jesus*."[140] The reason there is no Jew/Greek, slave/free, male/female is because the Galatians are one in Christ. It is impossible to fully appreciate Galatians 3–4, and consequently Galatians 3:28, without recognizing God's redemptive purposes, first promised to Abraham's one Seed and, in time, delivered to all people who are *in Christ*.

---

[137] Bartling, "New Creation," 412-413. For other examples of "in Christ" being used with a corporate emphasis, see Rom. 12:4; 1 Cor. 12:13ff.
[138] Beker, *Paul the Apostle*, 309-310.
[139] This could also be stated "all in one," as all believers are incorporated into the one Christ. The expression Beker uses, "one in all," is likewise true, as Christ is in all believers.
[140] Harris, "Prepositions," 3:1192, italics mine.

### The Meaning of the Three Negated Couplets

There is, of course, one question of great importance yet to be addressed in this section on verse 28: What is the meaning of "there is no male and female"? Or, put more broadly, what does Paul mean when he negates these three couplets? The reason for the negations as a whole is clear: It is because all the Galatians are "one in Christ Jesus." What Paul meant by each of the three negations, however, is not so self-evident. The purpose of this section is to offer a proposal regarding the meaning of the negations. A comprehensive summary of verse 28 will come in chapter 3.

What is the meaning of the negations of the three couplets? The couplets are in the form "there is no x or y."[141] It is clear that Paul did not intend this expression to literally mean "x and y do not exist"; no one believes Paul denied the existence of Jews, Greeks, slaves, free persons, males, and females. Even those who argue that the expression "there is no male or female" means there is no difference in male and female *roles* do not believe the negation "there is no male or female" means that there is no such entity as a male. Though the phrase οὐκ ἔνι is best translated "there is no . . . ," the expression "there is no x or y" is a figure of speech meant to communicate something other than the nonexistence of these categories.

Most of the proposals for the meaning of the expression "there is no Jew/Greek, slave/free, male/female" have suggested that Paul's use of this expression is intended to negate a distinction between these groups in some regard. Thus "there is no x or y" really means "there is no distinction between x and y." Paul obviously is not denying all distinctions between these groups, as he later notes distinctions, for example, between Jews and Gentiles. So what exactly is the meaning of "there is no x or y"? Unfortunately none of the other fifteen uses of the phrase

---

[141] It has already been acknowledged that the third couplet, οὐκ ἔνι ἄρσεν καὶ θῆλυ, is really of the form "there is no x *and* y." The switch from οὐδέ to καί is most likely done to refer to Genesis 1:27. Yet it is important not to place too much significance on the switch in conjunctions, as i) the couplets are all presented in a parallel manner, and ii) the parallel passage in Colossians 3:11 uses καί to join two couplets of opposites instead of οὐδέ, without any readily apparent change in meaning. As has already been argued, the best interpretation of this passage affirms a reference to Genesis 1:27 (in light of Paul's choice of rare nouns and his switch from οὐδέ to καί) and a translation that construes the couplets in a similar manner: "There is no Jew or Greek, slave or free, male or female." Longenecker agrees. See Richard L. Longenecker, *New Testament Social Ethics Today* (Grand Rapids, Mich.: Eerdmans, 1984), 75, note 6.

"there is no . . ."[142] in the 300 years surrounding the New Testament is similar to the uses in 3:28 ("there is no x or y"); so we must determine the meaning of this expression by examining its immediate context, as well as its broader biblical context. It would seem most probable that the phrase "there is no x or y . . ." is another way of saying "there is no distinction between x and y—*all* believers, regardless of their ethnic, religious, sexual, or economic state, are one in Christ." At least four different evidences suggest such an interpretation.

First, within Galatians 3:26-29 there is a clear emphasis on the *universal* nature of the benefits brought about by the advent of Christ: "You are *all* sons" (3:26), "for *all of you* who were baptized into Christ have clothed yourselves with Christ" (3:27), "for you are *all* one in Christ Jesus" (3:28). *All* who belong to Christ are sons and heirs. There is no Jew/Greek, slave/free, male/female *because* each and every person in these groups shares in Christ. If all people share in something R, then there is no distinction between these people insofar as their relationship to R is concerned. So the proposed meaning, "there is no distinction," fits the context well.

Second, Galatians 3:28 is part of a larger salvation-historical argument, and the Old Testament clearly anticipated that the new covenant would be universal, for all people. Paul writes that the Galatians are no longer minors but full sons, because the fullness of time has arrived (cf. Gal. 4:1-7). The new covenant age has appeared, and Gentiles and Jews are now heirs of the promise to Abraham. This event, as predicted by the Old Testament prophets Jeremiah and Joel, included the universal blessing of God on those who believe, whatever their place in life. Note:

> "This is the covenant I will make with the house of Israel after that time," declares the LORD. "I will put my law in their minds and write it on their hearts. I will be their God, and they will be my people. No longer will a man teach his neighbor, or a man his brother, saying, 'Know the LORD,' because they will *all* know me, *from the least to the greatest*," declares the LORD. (Jer. 31:33-34a, italics mine)

---

[142] Gk. οὐκ ἔνι

Here Jeremiah points to the universal nature of the new covenant; everyone, from the least to the greatest, will be able to know the Lord. Joel's prophetic description of the arrival of this day includes the same element:

> "And afterward I will pour out my Spirit on *all* people. Your sons and daughters will prophesy, your old men will dream dreams, your young men will see visions. Even on my servants, both men and women, I will pour out my Spirit in those days." (Joel 2:28-29, italics mine)

Joel, like Paul in Galatians 3:28, uses couplets of opposites to delineate "all people": "I will pour out my Spirit on *all* people . . . both *men* and *women.*" He describes all people by contrasting sons/daughters, old/young, men/women; *all* people will receive God's Spirit.

Jeremiah 31 and Joel 2 are important Old Testament descriptions of the arrival of the new covenant, the fulfillment of which is described in Galatians 3–4. These two Old Testament passages stress the universality of the new covenant by using couplets of opposites, much like the couplets found in Galatians 3:28. It is clear that phrases such as "from the least to the greatest" and "even on my servants, both men and women" are meant to include everybody, without distinction. The mere presence of universal language here in Galatians 3:26-29 does not, by itself, ensure a direct link from Galatians 3:28 to the Old Testament passages noted above. Likewise, there is no evidence that Paul was citing these Old Testament authors or that his expression "there is no x or y" is directly tied to Jeremiah's somewhat different phrase "from the least to the greatest" ("from x *to* y").

What is argued here is that:

- The anticipated new covenant blessing was universal, promised to all individuals who believed, without distinction: "*Whoever* calls on the name of the LORD will be delivered" (Joel 2:32, NASB). Furthermore, the promise to Abraham, which is *clearly* in view in Galatians 3–4, had a universal scope: "I will bless those who bless you, and *whoever* curses you I will curse; and *all* peoples on earth will be blessed through you" (Gen. 12:3; cf. Gen. 17:5).

- Galatians 3:28 describes the new covenant people of God who are recipients of the promise made to Abraham.

- Since the Old Testament prophecies (Jer. 31; Joel 2) and the promise to Abraham (Gen. 12) emphasized that all God's people would be included in the new covenant, and since Galatians 3:28 describes the people of the new covenant, it is reasonable to conclude that the formula "there is no x or y" has the same intent as what was predicted in the Old Testament; that is, that everybody is included, without distinction, from the least to the greatest (Jer. 31), men and women (Joel 2), old and young (Joel 2).

Third, interpreting "there is no x or y" as "there is no distinction . . . all are one" makes sense when considering that the New Testament often uses pairs of opposites as a literary device (called a "merism") to express the concept of totality or universality. Granted, pairs of opposites may have other functions (e.g., life/death, light/dark), but when the opposites consist of groups of people, these structures frequently denote *all* people. For example: "For we were *all* baptized by one Spirit into one body—whether Jews or Greeks, slave or free—and we were all given the one Spirit to drink" (1 Cor. 12:13). Here two pairs of opposites, Jew/Greek and slave/free, simply function in apposition to "all"; the pairs Jew/Greek and slave/free are another way of denoting "all people." Further examples of this include Revelation 19:18: ". . . so that you may eat the flesh of kings, generals, and mighty men, of horses and their riders, and the flesh of *all people,* free and slave, small and great"; and Ephesians 6:8: ". . . because you know the Lord will reward *everyone* for whatever good he does, whether he is slave or free" (italics mine). Also note Romans 10:11-12; 1 Corinthians 10:32; Colossians 3:11; Revelation 6:15.

The literary device of using opposites to denote universality is not limited to the Bible. Consider, for example, Martin Luther King, Jr.'s, famous "I Have a Dream" speech, delivered in front of the Lincoln Memorial in August 1963:

I have a dream my four little children will one day live in a nation
where they will not be judged by the color of their skin but by [the]
content of their character. . . . This will be the day when all God's children will be able to sing with new meaning—"my country 'tis of thee;
sweet land of liberty; of thee I sing; land where my fathers died, land
of the pilgrim's pride; from every mountain side, let freedom ring"—
and if America is to be a great nation, this must become true. So let
freedom ring. . . .

And when we allow freedom to ring, when we let it ring from
every village and hamlet, from every state and city, we will be able to
speed up the day when *all* of God's children—*black men and white
men, Jews and Gentiles, Catholics and Protestants*—will be able to
joins hands and sing the words of the old Negro spiritual, "Free at last,
free at last; thank God Almighty, we are free at last."[143]

Dr. King longed for the day when freedom would ring everywhere, when
*every* person would celebrate the emancipation of people of color from
racial discrimination. He chose pairs of opposites, black/white,
Jew/Gentile, Catholic/Protestant, to convey the universality of his dream.

Fourth, a comparison of Galatians 3:26-28 with similar Pauline passages confirms this proposed interpretation ("there is no distinction . . .
all are one"). Note the similarity between these first two passages and
3:26-28, which follows:

But now apart from the law the righteousness of God has been manifested, being witnessed by the Law and the Prophets, even the righteousness of God through faith in Jesus Christ for *all* those who
believe; for there is *no distinction*. . . . (Rom. 3:21-22, NASB, italics
mine)

For the Scripture says, "*Whoever* believes[144] in Him will not be dis-
appointed." For there is *no distinction* between Jew and Greek; for the
same Lord is Lord of *all*, abounding in riches for *all* who call upon
Him, for "*Whoever* will call upon the name of the Lord will be saved."
(Rom. 10:11-13, NASB, italics mine)

---

143 Martin Luther King, Jr., "I Have a Dream" (speech given in Washington, D.C., August 28,
1963), in *A Testament of Hope: The Essential Writings of Martin Luther King, Jr.,* ed. James
Melvin Washington (San Francisco: Harper & Row, 1986), 219-220, italics mine.
144 Gk. πᾶς ὁ πιστεύων

For you are *all* sons of God through faith in Christ Jesus. For *all* of you who were baptized into Christ have clothed yourselves with Christ. There is neither Jew nor Greek, there is neither slave nor free man, there is neither male nor female; for you are *all* one in Christ Jesus. (Gal. 3:26-28, NASB, italics mine)

Several common themes are repeated in all three of these passages:

- All three passages occur in a salvation-historical context.

- There is an unmistakable universal emphasis; the blessings of God are available to *all* who are in his Son, regardless of human distinctions.

- Each passage refers to the inclusion of the Gentiles. Although the first passage cited above (Rom. 3:21-22) contains no mention of the Gentiles, just after these verses, in the same thought unit, Paul writes, "Is God the God of Jews only? Is he not the God of Gentiles too? Yes, of Gentiles too, since there is only one God, who will justify the circumcised by faith and the uncircumcised through that same faith" (Rom 3:29-30).

- Though many different expressions are used, there is a repeated emphasis on believing in Christ: ". . . through faith in Jesus Christ for all those who believe" (Rom. 3:22, NASB); "whoever believes . . . all who call upon Him" (Rom. 10:11-12, NASB); "through faith in Christ Jesus" (Gal. 3:26).

- The Jew/Greek couplet used in Galatians 3:28[145] is used in much the same manner as in Romans 10:12. Of even greater interest is that Romans 10:12 *directly* cites Joel 2:28-32. In Romans Paul's intent is not clouded by the ambiguous "there is no x or y" as in Galatians 3:28, but his use of this couplet here is clear: There is *no distinction* between Jew and Greek—all who call upon him will be saved. If Galatians 3:28 is tied to Joel 2:28-32, which seems likely, then given the use

---

[145] Gk. Ἰουδαίος/ Ἕλλην

of the Jew/Greek couplet in Romans 10:12, the meaning of "there is no x or y" in Galatians 3:28 is, "There is no distinction between x and y." That is, all believers, without distinction, are one in Christ.

In summary, while the lexical data establishes a literal translation of the phrase οὐκ ἔνι [NIV, "there is neither] as "there is no x or y," numerous contextual clues, as argued above, provide evidence that this phrase is a figure of speech meant to communicate universality—"there is no distinction between x and y," *all* believers are one in Christ.

Once a suitable interpretation is found for the enigmatic "there is no x or y," one might hope that there would be agreement on the meaning of Galatians 3:28. This is not the case. In fact, the wide gulf that separates complementarians and egalitarians on Galatians 3:28 is reflected in differing positions regarding what is meant by "there is no distinction" between Jew/Greek, slave/free, male/female. We will look at this issue in the next chapter.

Verse 28, then, consists of three couplets of polar opposites, each of which functions as a merism to refer universally to all people. Paul affirms that all believers, without distinction, are united to one Christ and are therefore one with each other. Being united to the one Christ is essential for many reasons, as verse 29 clarifies. A complete summary of verse 28 is the task for the next chapter.

## GALATIANS 3:29

The NIV presents verse 29 as if it were a conditional clause followed by two phrases joined by the conjunction *and:* "If you belong to Christ, then you are Abraham's seed, *and* heirs according to the promise." But the second phrase is actually epexegetic to the first, as in the NASB: "If you belong to Christ, then you are Abraham's offspring, heirs according to the promise." Being Abraham's seed is concomitant with being an heir to the promise.

### *"If you belong to Christ, . . ."*

The expression "belong to Christ" reiterates the preceding "in Christ Jesus" (v. 28). Betz comments, "In 3:29, the conditional protasis sums up 3:26-28 by now using the genitive construction 'to be Christ's' instead of the expression 'in Christ Jesus.' This shows that the two phrases are not different in meaning."[146] Being in Christ is the same as belonging to Christ.

*"... then you are Abraham's seed, and heirs according to the promise."*
The conclusion "then you are Abraham's seed, and heirs according to the promise" serves as more than just the apodosis of the conditional statement in verse 29; this conclusion indeed ties together the argument based on Abraham that began in 3:6. Paul started by pointing to Abraham's faith (Gen. 15) and recounting the promise made to Abraham (Gen. 12). He then explained that the promises given to Abraham and his seed referred to Christ, "through whom the promised blessing was to come to all the Gentiles."[147] In an odd twist on the word "seed," Paul now explains that all those in Christ, regardless of whether or not they are physical descendants of Abraham, are heirs of the promise made to Abraham.

*Seed*[148] is a collective noun.[149] As a collective noun it is found predominantly in the singular (e.g., Matt. 13:24), and only rarely in the plural (Matt. 13:32; Mark 4:31; 1 Cor. 15:38; and Gal. 3:16). Paul's argument in Galatians 3:16 plays upon the collective sense of this word. "The promises were spoken to Abraham and to his seed," which, given the collective nature of this noun, could naturally be interpreted as meaning "to those [plural] who were Abraham's faith descendants." But Paul points to the singular form[150] rather than the plural[151] as being the crux of the Old Testament teaching: Abraham's "seed" was singular, therefore Abraham's seed was Christ. Paul cleverly uses "seed" two ways in Galatians 3–4: Used in a singular sense, the term ties the promise made to Abraham to Christ; used as a collective term, it represents those who are in Christ (who are Abraham's seed—singular)[152] and heirs according to the promise (plural).

---

[146] Betz, *Galatians*, 201. The two expressions Χριστοῦ and ἐν Χριστῷ Ἰησοῦ could have different nuances in different contexts. Here, however, they have the same meaning.
[147] Bruce, *Galatians*, 172.
[148] Gk. σπέρμα
[149] Just like the Hebrew זֶרַע
[150] Gk. σπέρματι
[151] Gk. σπέρμασιν
[152] Burton notes the lack of the article here (cf. 3:16). "Paul does not say to his readers, 'Ye are *the* seed of Abraham,' as he might perhaps have done ... [rather] σπέρμα, being without the arti-

*Promise*[153] and *inheritance*[154] are rich theological terms that are conceptually related. An heir, by definition, stands to inherit something; the inheritance received by those who belong to Yahweh is often described in Scripture as that which was promised by God.[155] Because the inheritance is promised by God, it is something that God's people confidently expect, and it is also something for which they eagerly yearn. Both of these terms (*promise* and *inheritance*) are critical concepts in portraying God's plan throughout salvation-history. Indeed, it would be difficult to understand the biblical story line, from the earliest parts of Genesis on, without understanding *promise* and *inheritance*.

Not surprisingly, Galatians 3–4, with its explanation of salvation-history from Abraham to Christ, is replete with references to the promise and to the concept of heir/inheritance.[156] Generally "promise" is found in the singular, as here in verse 29.[157] It commonly appears without a preposition, but four times in Galatians, including 3:29, it is tied to a preposition.[158] From the uses in Galatians we can make several observations regarding this promise: i) the promise includes the Holy Spirit (3:14); ii) the promises were given to Abraham (3:16); iii) the promise is based on a covenant and not on the law (3:17); iv) the content of the promise includes the inheritance (3:18); v) the promise was given in grace, by God, to Abraham (3:18); vi) the promise is given through faith in Jesus Christ (3:22); vii) the promise was given *to* Jesus Christ (3:19, NASB);[159] viii) those who are in Christ receive the promise (3:29); and ix) Christians are children of the promise (4:28).

---

cle, is indefinite or qualitative. It may designate its subject [those who belong to Christ] as included in the seed (as distinguished from constituting it, which would have required the article)." Burton, *Galatians*, 209, italics mine.

[153] Gk. ἐπαγγελία

[154] Gk. κληρονόμος

[155] See for example these two ideas together in Rom. 4:13-14; Heb. 6:17; James 2:5.

[156] Ἐπαγγελία (promise) occurs ten times in these two chapters: Gal. 3:14, 16, 17, 18 (2x), 21, 22, 29; 4:23, 28. Κληρονόμος (heir) is found in 3:29; 4:1, 7. Κληρονομία (inheritance) occurs in Gal. 3:18. Similar concepts are expressed with other terms. Note, for example, these expressions that convey the notion of an inheritance: "did you *receive* the Spirit"; "does God *give* you his Spirit"; "so those who have faith are *blessed* along with Abraham"; "the *blessing* given to Abraham might come to the Gentiles." Italics mine.

[157] Exceptions in Galatians 3–4 are 3:16 and 3:21.

[158] 3:18a, ἐξ ἐπαγγελίας; 3:18b and 4:23, δι' ἐπαγγελίας; and 3:29, κατ' ἐπαγγελίαν. A. Sand, "ἐπαγγελία," *EDNT*, 2:14.

[159] The NIV has "until the Seed to whom the promise referred had come." This misses the fact that the promise didn't simply *refer* to the Seed, but was *made* to the Seed. Note NASB, "until the seed should come to whom the promise had been made"; Longenecker, "until the Seed for whom the promise was intended should come," Longenecker, *Galatians*, 138; and Burton, "to continue until

While much is forthrightly observable about the promise, several puzzling questions remain unanswered: What exactly is the content of the promise?[160] When, and to whom, was the promise given? And how, precisely, is the promise fulfilled? Complete answers to these questions are not necessary for our study on Galatians 3:28, but the following observations are pertinent:

i) The promise is here now (3:22, 29). Paul's emphasis in Galatians 3–4 is on the present—it is a contrast between "then" and "now," rather than between "now" and "yet to come."[161] If one belongs to Christ, one is presently an heir according to the promise (3:29). The verb is in the present tense: "You *are* Abraham's seed, heirs according to the promise." This is not to deny that there are future elements of the promise. Furthermore, this is not to deny that in other places Paul describes the Spirit as a down payment for what is to come (2 Cor. 5:5). It is, rather, to highlight that, in Galatians 3–4, the focus is on the present arrival of the promise/inheritance.

ii) The promise *is* the Spirit (3:14). The plural references ("promises," 3:16, 21) can be explained in two satisfactory ways: Either the promise was repeated on numerous occasions and/or in different forms, which could result in the plural form;[162] or the promise (singular), which is the Spirit, had other facets, such as changes in a believer's relationship to the law, becoming a child of God (4:1-7), etc. Thus, the arrival of the Spirit (the promise) brought about the fulfillment of many promises. This second explanation seems most probable.

iii) The promise was given to Abraham (3:16, 18), to Christ (3:16, 19), and to those who belong to Christ (3:22, 29; 4:7).[163] Note how

---

the seed should come to whom the promise still in force was made," Burton, *Galatians,* 189. The promise was made *to* Christ.

[160] Sam Williams lists the different options held by scholars. See Sam K. Williams, "*Promise* in Galatians: A Reading of Paul's Reading of Scripture," *JBL* 107 (1988): 709, n. 2.

[161] Ibid., 711-712.

[162] See Burton, *Galatians,* 181; and Williams, "*Promise* in Galatians," 712.

[163] If the promise *is* the Spirit, in what sense is the promise given to Christ? Williams makes a case which, though not important for our purposes, is nonetheless intriguing. He argues that Paul's citation "and to your seed" must come from Genesis 13:15 or 17:8, both references to the land. Paul, Williams argues, would not have understood "land" as simply Canaan, but as a type for the

beautifully Galatians 3:29 summarizes what has gone before. Each of the three groups who were to receive the promise—Christ, Abraham, and those who are in Christ—are pulled together: "If you belong to Christ, then you are Abraham's seed, and heirs according to the promise."

## SUMMARY OF GALATIANS 3:26-29

Galatians 3:26-29 is the climax of Paul's argument that began with his report of the Antioch incident (2:11-14). Failing to understand the changes that resulted from the arrival of Christ, the Gentile Galatians were susceptible to the false teaching that they must somehow be related to the ways of Abraham and the law-covenant in order to be true heirs. Their confusion is understandable. Since the Old Testament tied the promise and its blessings to being of the seed of Abraham, the Gentile Galatians, lacking a connection to Abraham, could easily conclude that it would be impossible for them to become heirs of the promise without doing something to be tied to Abraham. Now, however, says Paul, God has made sonship and the inheritance available to all who are in Christ.

The inheritance is still dependent on being related to Abraham. What has changed, however, is that now one becomes a seed of Abraham by being related to *the* Seed of Abraham, Jesus Christ, through faith. So the inheritance is now available to Jew and Greek alike:

> Christians are the seed of Abraham because they are "one in Christ" (Gal. 3.28b) who is the true seed of Abraham. All those who are in Christ are the seed of Abraham whether they be Jew or Gentile. For Paul, as well as for the rest of the New Testament, the concept of Inheritance is Christocentric. Christ is the true Seed from whom the rest of the spiritual descendants of the Promise spring.[164]

---

world. "Thus, as Paul reads the Abraham story, God promised the world to Abraham and to his single seed, Christ." Then Williams views "land" as not merely geographical area, but sovereign rule: "My thesis is that Paul has in mind not the possession of real estate but the exercise of authority." In order to see this happen, Williams argues, the Spirit is necessary to make Gentiles children of God and bring about the submission of all to Christ. So, the Spirit is, in this sense, promised to Christ. Hence, according to Williams, the singular promise is simply the Spirit, without other entailments. The promised Spirit is promised to Abraham, to Christ, and to all believers. Williams, "*Promise* in Galatians," 709-720.

[164] James D. Hester, *Paul's Concept of Inheritance: A Contribution to the Understanding of Heilsgeschichte*, Scottish Journal of Theology Occasional Papers, no. 14 (Edinburgh: Oliver and Boyd, 1968), 51.

Sandwiched between verses 26 and 29, Galatians 3:28 describes God's people in the new covenant. These people have fully associated with Christ; they have been baptized into him and have clothed themselves with him. By nature of their incorporation into him, they have become the rightful heirs of the blessing promised to Abraham, and sons of God. As predicted by the Old Testament, the new covenant is now known by its universal call; *all* are invited, whether Jew or Greek, slave or free, male or female. There is no distinction in God's people; no race, nation, class, or gender has favored status with God. As the old revival preacher used to say, "The ground is level at the foot of the cross." Every member of God's household enters the same way, by being related to God's Son. And because all of God's family shares in his one Son, there is now a new unity among God's people.

Several important issues regarding Galatians 3:28 have yet to be discussed. The next chapter addresses those issues and presents a comprehensive interpretation that incorporates the exegetical work done in chapters 1 and 2.

# 3

# THE MEANING AND SIGNIFICANCE
# OF GALATIANS 3:28

With the necessary exegetical groundwork laid, I will now put forth and defend an interpretation of Galatians 3:28 that I believe best fits the evidence. I will do so by first summarizing the two most popularly held positions on Galatians 3:28 and then, through interaction with these positions, offering an alternative interpretation. Before we begin, however, it will be helpful to make four observations about the structure and content of Galatians 3:28 that are essential for any proper interpretation of this verse.

## FOUR STRUCTURAL OBSERVATIONS ABOUT GALATIANS 3:28

i) The structure of this verse, with three parallel couplets, dictates that these couplets be interpreted together. This does not mean that we ignore the change in conjunctions from the first two couplets to the third couplet;[1] as mentioned previously, the third couplet likely refers to Genesis 1:27. Given, however, the parallel structure of the three couplets, it is best to translate the final couplet in the same way as the first two.

Though the couplets are presented in a parallel manner, and need to be interpreted in this way, there are nevertheless foundational differences between them. For example, the couplets differ in respect to the fall. The slave/free distinction resulted from the fall, but the Jew/Gentile distinction, as well as the male/female distinction, were not the result of the fall. Those who argue, then, that the arrival of Christ reversed the effects of the fall

---

[1] Gk. from οὐδέ to καί

and, correspondingly, reversed the polarities of Jew/Greek, slave/free, male/female start from the wrong presupposition. Each of these three couplets is related to the fall in a unique manner, and hence redemption has a unique effect on each couplet. M. E. Glasswell is correct in his comment: "The three pairs do not have precisely the same significance if one looks at other places where Paul discusses them separately. The differences within each pair are seen as being overcome in Christ but not abolished completely, though this is true of each pair differently."[2]

Colin Kruse, investigating human relationships in the Pauline epistles, comes to a similar conclusion. Kruse examined Paul's treatment of six pairs of human relationships throughout the Pauline corpus: Jew/Gentile, master/slave, male/female, husband/wife, parent/child, and citizen/state. He concludes:

> No common pattern emerges as far as the retention in principle of all six human relationships surveyed is concerned. On the one hand, theological support was *not* offered for the retention in principle of Jew-Gentile and slave-master relationships. On the other hand, however, theological reasons *were* provided which imply the necessity of the retention in principle of the male-female, husband-wife, parent-child and citizen-state relationships.[3]

The conclusions of Glasswell and Kruse are helpful for the study of Galatians 3:28, for if Paul treats the couplets of Jew/Greek, slave/free, and male/female differently elsewhere in the Pauline corpus, one should be reticent to insist that these couplets be treated in an identical manner in Galatians 3:28.

Some have argued that the Jew/Greek paradigm should be used to interpret the other two couplets. Since there is no distinction between Jew and Gentile in the church (cf. 2:11-14), it is argued, then there should be no distinction between men and women in the church either.[4]

---

[2] M. E. Glasswell, "Some Issues of Church and Society in Light of Paul's Eschatology," in *Paul and Paulinism: Essays in Honour of C. K. Barrett,* eds. M. D. Hooker and S. G. Wilson (London: SPCK, 1982), 315.

[3] Colin Kruse, "Human Relationships in the Pauline Corpus," in *The Fullness of Time: Biblical Studies in Honour of Archbishop Donald Robinson,* eds. David Peterson and John Pryor (Homebush West, NSW: Lancer, 1992), 180.

[4] "If in ordinary life existence in Christ is manifested openly in church fellowship, then, if a Gentile may exercise spiritual leadership in church as freely as a Jew, or a slave as freely as a citizen, why not a woman as freely as a man?" F. F. Bruce, *The Epistle to the Galatians,* New International

But this type of argument is an example of ignoring the differences between the couplets. Hypothetically, using similar reasoning, someone might use the slave/free couplet as a paradigm for the male/female couplet. Then it could be said that because Paul affirms that slaves should obey their masters, all Gentiles should obey Jews and all women should obey men. No sane person argues that this should be the case, but such an example shows the danger of arbitrarily using one couplet to explain the other when the couplets are fundamentally different.

In summary, the couplets differ in respect to the fall, in respect to redemption, and in their essence, and Paul treats these couplets differently throughout his letters. Here, in Galatians 3:28, these couplets are presented in series, in a parallel fashion. This structure does not imply that Paul thought each couplet was the same, but rather that something tied them together; in some way they are similar. To insist that the couplets are the same is a mistake; likewise it is an error to insist that they are independent. They are parallel.

ii) The couplets must be interpreted in light of the reason Paul gives for their negation. There is no Jew/Greek, slave/free, male/female *because* they are all one in Christ. The phrase "you are all one in Christ Jesus" is quite important, as it is the reason Paul himself gives for his negation of the couplets.[5]

---

Greek Testament Commentary (Grand Rapids, Mich.: Eerdmans, 1982), 190. Snodgrass, however, admits that the male/female distinction is different than the Jew/Greek couplet: "With regard to male/female relationships, the situation is different because it deals with the obvious physical distinction of sexuality." Klyne Snodgrass, "Galatians 3:28: Conundrum or Solution?" *Women, Authority, and the Bible* (Downers Grove, Ill.: InterVarsity, 1986), 176. Interestingly, while Snodgrass admits that the three couplets are different, he comments on the motives of others who do so: "Still, some people point out that the three categories are not alike. One is religious, one is social, and one is sexual. Often, but not necessarily, this observation is linked to an attempt to maintain a hierarchical relation of the sexes." Ibid., 175. Regardless of one's interpretative biases or motives, it seems clear that these pairs are inherently different.
[5] If one interprets the negation of the couplets in light of some reason other than the one Paul provided, a plethora of colorful interpretations can emerge. For example, in 2 Clement 12, 1-6, there is a saying that resembles Galatians 3:28. Clement, in explaining a "saying of the Lord" writes, "And by 'the male with the female neither male nor female' he means this, that when a brother sees a sister he should have no thought of her as female, nor she of him as male." *The Apostolic Fathers* 1, Loeb Classical Library (London: William Heinemann, 1965), 147-149. If Clement is referring to Galatians 3:28 (and this is less than certain), his interpretation would be an example of failing to consider properly the rationale Paul himself provided for the negations. The reason Paul gives for why there is no male or female is because all are one in Christ Jesus. If "oneness in Christ" can be shown to be the ground for why men and women should have pure (neuter?) thoughts of each other, then Clement's interpretation could be a viable option. But it seems more likely that Clement has failed to consider the reason Paul himself offered for the negations, resulting in an interpretation that strays from the intent of Galatians 3–4 and Galatians 3:28. I cite this

iii) The paragraph 3:26-29 is clearly framed by the two phrases "you are all sons of God" (v. 26), and (therefore) "you are Abraham's seed, . . . heirs according to the promise" (v. 29). Verse 28 is a piece of a larger argument, and any interpretation must reflect this as well. Daniel Fuller notes,

> The third statement, Galatians 3:28, comes between two climactic affirmations of the blessings enjoyed by faith in Christ. "In Christ Jesus you are all sons of God, through faith. For as many of you as were baptized into Christ have put on Christ" (vv. 27f.). Afterwards comes the affirmation, "If you are Christ's then you are Abraham's offspring, heirs according to the promise" (v. 29). Therefore the negations of v. 28—neither Jew nor Greek, neither bond nor free, neither male nor female—want to deny that the blessings of being united with Christ depend in any way upon race, class, or gender.[6]

iv) The couplets must be interpreted in light of the salvation-historical flow of Galatians 3-4. As previously mentioned, Galatians 3:26-29 and Galatians 3:28 are part of a larger argument. Any suggested interpretation of the couplets should fit the context of the entire book.

Proponents of both sides of the gender dispute would probably agree on the importance of these four structural observations, which flow from the text.

We will now examine the two most commonly held interpretations of Galatians 3:28, which I will refer to as the "egalitarian" and "complementarian" positions. Although both of these terms are laden with many ideas not specifically found in Galatians 3:28, I will use them nonetheless, because they serve as convenient, well-recognized labels.

## THE TWO MAJOR INTERPRETATIONS OF GALATIANS 3:28

Generally speaking there are two major interpretations offered today for the phrase "there is no male or female." Did Paul intend Galatians 3:28

---

example simply to illustrate the importance of interpreting the negations in Galatians 3:28 in light of the reason Paul has provided in the text.

[6] Daniel P. Fuller, "Paul and Galatians 3:28," *Theological Students Bulletin* 9, no. 2 (1985): 9. Fuller rightly recognizes that Galatians 3:28 is sandwiched between two key phrases found in 3:26 and 3:29, and that these phrases must inform any interpretation of Galatians 3:28. His conclusions, however, on the meaning and significance of Galatians 3:28 differ from those in this thesis.

to be the "most socially explosive statement in the New Testament,"[7] teaching that there should be few or no distinctions in gender roles for God's people in the new age? This is the egalitarian position. Or, as complementarians argue, was Paul's primary emphasis that there is no distinction between individuals in these groups of people when it comes to becoming heirs of the promise and sons of God?

### An Egalitarian Interpretation

Though there are small differences among egalitarians,[8] it is nevertheless possible to summarize succinctly their position. This section will cite at length representative egalitarian scholars to allow them to present their position.

Egalitarians believe that Galatians 3:28 represents the new breaking in upon the old. Snodgrass comments:

> The issue is not merely that all are accepted by God on the same terms. The point that the text makes is that something new has come into being in Christ. . . . If the new age has broken in, we cannot allow ourselves to continue to be determined by the old. . . . Whatever else is done with the other texts concerning women, justice must be done to the newness proclaimed in Gal 3:28.[9]

Furthermore, according to egalitarians, this new age has not only wrought theological changes, i.e., the inclusion of the Gentiles or the arrival of the Spirit, but these theological changes are manifested in sociological changes as well.[10] Longenecker states, "The most forthright

---

[7] Snodgrass, "Galatians 3:28," 161.

[8] In this section I will try to present a strong, fair case for egalitarianism, allowing major, credible spokespersons for this position to present their case. I will mention a couple of minor differences among egalitarians. It is possible, though not common, to be an egalitarian without building one's argument on Galatians 3:28. Craig Keener, for example, makes only three references to Galatians 3:28 in his book *Paul, Women and Wives*. Given that his entire book is devoted to Paul's teaching on women and wives, this is a remarkably small number. Perhaps this scarcity of references indicates that Keener does not believe Galatians 3:28 is a critical Pauline text on the roles of women and wives. Craig Keener, *Paul, Women and Wives* (Peabody, Mass: Hendrickson, 1992).

[9] Snodgrass, "Galatians 3:28," 175, 178.

[10] Some egalitarians claim that the arrival of Christ and the new covenant has brought about *theological* changes, but the concomitant *sociological* changes are only manifested over time. They recognize that the NT didn't absolutely ban slavery, but, they argue, over time the church realized that the NT certainly contained the foundational truth to eventually overthrow slavery. The case for women's roles is then argued in a manner parallel to slavery. Just as slavery was eradicated over time, now gender roles in the home and church should be eliminated. Arguments such as this are based on "trajectory hermeneutics." The Bible says something, but because we know

statement on social ethics in all the New Testament is found in Galatians 3:28."[11] Thus, the expression "there is no Jew or Greek" means that not only have things changed in redemptive history with Jews and Greeks, but, as a result, things have changed socially, affecting relationships between Jews and Greeks. Boomsma comments, "The basis for Galatians 3:28 is the vertical relationship with God and the believer taught in verses 26-27. The *primary* focus of verse 28 is the horizontal relationships of the Christian community."[12] Each group of people, then, has experienced a change in *status* that has resulted in new *roles*. It is an error of great magnitude, according to this argument, to recognize solely the theological changes—that is, changes in status—without recognizing the sociological implications as well. As Snodgrass insists,

> Without attempting to deny the distinctions between the sexes, we err greatly if we do not insist on equal standing for women with men in Christ. To deny the social implications of this text is a ploy that will not work. Nothing about the Christian faith may be labeled "merely *coram Deo*" ("in the eyes of God"), and I do not know any other subject on which people argue in this fashion.[13]

Women in the past have been second-class citizens, it is argued, both in society and in the church. Now, however, they "have the same status as children of God"[14] and are one in Christ with men:

---

its trajectory, we can see how we should act differently now. It is not uncommon to find scholars arguing this way. See, for example, Richard L. Longenecker, *New Testament Social Ethics Today* (Grand Rapids, Mich.: Eerdmans, 1984); and David L Thompson, "Women, Men, Slaves and the Bible: Hermeneutical Inquiries," in *Christian Scholar's Review* 25 (1996). Problems arise, however, when someone argues for a position, based on a trajectory, that contradicts what is written in a biblical text. Wayne Grudem comments on David Thompson's article: "Thompson agrees that Ephesians 5 and Colossians 3 teach male headship (p. 330) but tells us that we can go beyond that today: He says the Biblical authors were moving in a 'trajectory' toward an egalitarian . . . position but they didn't quite get there by the time of 'the last entry in the biblical conversation' (p. 339). We can accept the target they were moving toward and affirm an egalitarian position today (p. 339) even if it isn't explicitly taught in Scripture." Wayne Grudem, "Asbury Professor Advocates Egalitariansim But Undermines Biblical Authority," in *CBMW News*, vol. 2, no. 1 (December 1996), 8. See also Yarbrough's critique of Stendahl's similar hermeneutic. Robert W. Yarbrough, "The Hermeneutics of 1 Timothy 2:9-15," in *Women in the Church: A Fresh Analysis of 1 Timothy 2:9-15*, eds. Andreas J. Köstenberger, Thomas R. Schreiner, and H. Scott Baldwin (Grand Rapids, Mich.: Baker, 1995), 178ff. Not all egalitarians use "trajectory hermeneutics." Many believe Galatians 3:28 in its NT context teaches that there are no longer gender-based roles in the home and church. For these scholars, there is no need to apply "trajectory hermeneutics."
[11] Longenecker, *New Testament Social Ethics*, 30.
[12] Clarence Boomsma, *Male and Female, One in Christ: New Testament Teaching on Women in Office* (Grand Rapids, Mich.: Baker, 1993), 36, italics mine.
[13] Snodgrass, "Galatians 3:28," 178-179.
[14] Ibid., 174.

Gentiles, slaves and women are granted access and standing in Christ on the same footing and with the same valuation, privileges and responsibilities as Jewish and free men. . . . While not answering all our questions about the roles of women in society, Galatians 3:28 prohibits the valuations and divisions of the old order and insists on equal standing and unity in Christ.[15]

So the arrival of the new has wrought changes in both status and roles,[16] bringing "equal standing" for Gentiles, slaves, and women. The improvements ushered in for each group "react against the old valuations."[17] The phrase "there is no male or female" means "there are no distinctions between men and women—both have the same standing and roles."

While insisting that women have the same standing and roles as men, egalitarians nevertheless are careful to acknowledge that the new age has not obliterated differences between men and women. Rather "the alienating and divisive effects of sin associated with the distinctions of nationality, social status, and gender are erased for those who are in Christ."[18] Sexual differences still remain from creation, but these "are immaterial to equality in the life of the church. [Instead] the equality of people's potential for worth, function [i.e., roles], responsibility, and authority lies in unity with Christ, which is not restricted by their ethnicity, social status, or gender."[19]

There are some minor variations among egalitarians. Most, for example, see "male headship" as a result of the fall. Correspondingly, this headship is then eradicated by redemption, which is described, in part, in Galatians 3:28. Thus, redemption *restores* creation. Longenecker and Grenz, however, see redemption as going *beyond* creation. Longenecker writes,

---

[15] Ibid., 178, 180.
[16] While all egalitarians believe that Christ and the new era have brought about changes in women's roles, some egalitarians, such as Klyne Snodgrass, do not believe that this new era has changed marriage roles in such a way as to eradicate the unique roles of husbands and wives.
[17] Ibid., 178.
[18] Boomsma, *Male and Female*, 38.
[19] Ibid. Note that Boomsma directly roots "equality" between men and women in "unity in Christ." The relationship between Galatians 3:28 and equality will be discussed later in this chapter.

Because of creation there are differences between the sexes which exist for the blessing of both men and women for the benefit of society. Paul does not argue for anything like unisexuality or some supposed androgynous ideal. Heterosexuality is presupposed in all of his letters as having been ordained by God, and he has nothing but contempt and condemnation for homosexual practices. Yet Paul also lays emphasis on redemption in such a way as to indicate what God has done in Christ *transcends* what is true simply of creation.[20]

To be more specific Longenecker says elsewhere:

Paul and his colleagues seem to have been working from two important categories of thought: that category of thought which emphasizes what God has done through creation, wherein order, subordination, and submission are generally stressed, and that category which emphasizes what God has done redemptively, wherein freedom, mutuality, and equality take prominence.[21]

Stanley Grenz sounds similar to Longenecker:

Even if God had built this principle [male headship] into creation from the beginning (which we have already indicated is not the case), this would not necessarily require that the Church continue to practice male leadership and female subordination. *Christ did not establish the Church merely to be the mirror of original creation but to anticipate the eschatological new community.* We are to live in accordance with the principles of God's new creation and thereby reflect the character of the triune God.[22]

Longenecker and Grenz are representative of egalitarians who believe that the redemption provided by Christ goes beyond the created order. Correspondingly, these egalitarians would argue, sexual roles that were established as part of the original order have changed. The new era is a time of mutuality, equality, and freedom, in contrast to the old era, which was a time of subordination and submission.[23]

---

[20] Longenecker, *New Testament Social Ethics*, 92, italics mine.
[21] Ibid., 84.
[22] Stanley Grenz, "Anticipating God's New Community: Theological Foundations for Women in Ministry," *Journal of the Evangelical Theological Society* 38 (1995): 604, italics mine.
[23] At the end of the day, egalitarians who argue that redemption *restores* creation and those who argue that redemption *goes beyond* creation both end up affirming that the present era is a time

In summary, egalitarians are particularly interested in highlighting the sociological implications of Galatians 3:28. They see substantial changes in the shift from the old covenant to the new, even if they disagree on the specifics of how redemption relates to creation. The arrival of the new age has shattered old patterns of racial, sexual, and class discrimination and has brought about a new existence in Christ, where everyone is one in Christ and has equal opportunity, regardless of race, class, or sex.[24]

## A Complementarian Interpretation

Complementarians are even more monolithic than egalitarians, so summarizing their position on Galatians 3:28 is a relatively straightforward task. As in the egalitarian summary, this section will allow complementarians to speak for themselves.

Complementarians believe Galatians 3:28, understood in its con-

---

when the roles of men and women in the home and church are interchangeable. Though there are some strains of truth in Longenecker's and Grenz's position, several points need clarification:

1) Their claim that redemption transcends creation is true. For example, in the consummate age believers will have resurrection bodies (1 Cor. 15) and people will "neither marry nor be given in marriage" (Matt. 22:30). Both of these changes transcend the created order. Neither of them, however, is presently true. This is because we currently live *between* the ages. One cannot assume that consummated Christian ethics are the norm for today, in every respect, when we are not yet in the consummate age. It is doubtful, for example, that either Grenz or Longenecker would agree that marriage is an invalid institution in today's age. The question, then, becomes this: Given that we are between the ages, and given that the era of the new covenant has brought about changes in the old, how then do we determine sexual roles between the ages? The answer to this question is that God's Word both prescribes and describes life between the ages. Texts such as Ephesians 5, Colossians 3, 1 Timothy 2, etc., are given to this end. Grenz's statement that the Church should not merely mirror creation but anticipate the new eschatological community is partly true: the church has the Spirit of God as a down payment; in this sense, and in others, it *does* transcend creation and anticipate the new community. But the church is not yet in the consummate age; it must await the day when creation is finally transformed. Because of this one cannot read *en toto* the ethics of the consummate age into this age.

2) Longenecker and Grenz are right when they insist that the new era *does* bring about substantial changes in the old. Paul does emphasize freedom (e.g., Gal. 5), mutuality (e.g., 1 Cor. 7), and equality (depending upon what is meant by equality). But the question remains: Do Paul and the rest of the NT writers describe the new era, i.e., our present life between the ages, as being a sharp break with creation? The answer to this appears to be no. On the contrary, Paul views the present redemption as including the restoration of creation (cf. Col. 3:10). Ben Witherington cites his mentor Andrew Lincoln on this: "All of this should immediately make us suspicious of any interpretation of Paul which makes a sharp distinction between creation and new creation: in Paul, redemption presupposes creation and includes creation (cf. Rom. 8.18ff.; Col. 1.20; Eph. 1.10), and Christ as Lord is mediator of both creation and redemption (cf. 1 Cor. 8.6)." Ben Witherington III, "Rite and Rights for Women," *New Testament Studies* 27 (1981): 598.

3) Furthermore, when Paul deals with sexual roles he often grounds his teaching by appealing to the created order (e.g., 1 Cor. 11:8; Eph. 5:31; 1 Tim. 2:13). This in itself should make one wary of affirming that sexual roles in the present are a radical break with sexual roles at creation. One cannot simply appeal to the fact that redemption transcends creation as proof that there are undifferentiated roles for men and women in the home and church in this life between the ages.

[24] Gilbert Bilezikian, *Beyond Sex Roles* (Grand Rapids, Mich.: Baker, 1985), 128.

text, is primarily concerned with the inclusion of all people "in the Abrahamic covenant with its attendant blessings."[25] Though not denying possible sociological implications, complementarians see Paul's emphasis as primarily theological. Burton[26] states:

> With the thought of the basis of acceptance with God in mind, expressed in v. 26 in the form that through faith men become sons of God, and in v. 27 in a different form, the sweep of his thought carries him [Paul] beyond the strict limits of the question at issue in Galatia to affirm that all distinctions are abolished, and to present an inspiring picture of the world under one universal religion. . . . It is only in the religion of Christ that Paul conceives that men can thus be brought together. *That he is speaking of these distinctions from the point of view of religion is evident from the context in general, but especially from his inclusion of the ineradicable distinction of sex. The passage has nothing to do directly with the merging of nationalities or the abolition of slavery.* . . . Yet that the principle had its indirect social significance is shown in the implications of the Antioch incident 2:11-14, and in Phm. 15, 16, Col. 4:1.[27]

In essence, this is the complementarian position: Galatians 3:28 is primarily about the inclusion of all peoples in the blessings of God in Christ. To use this verse for other purposes is illegitimate. Fung comments, "Paul's statement is not concerned with the role relationships of men and women within the Body of Christ but rather with their common initiation/integration into it through faith and baptism."[28]

---

[25] John Jefferson Davis, "Some Reflections on Galatians 3:28, Sexual Roles, and Biblical Hermeneutics," *Journal of the Evangelical Theological Society* 19 (1976): 202.

[26] Burton made Galatians his lifework for a quarter of a century, and his commentary, published in 1921, is the most comprehensive work on Galatians. His conclusions certainly place him in the complementarian camp, though he says very little related to the egalitarian/complementarian dispute over Galatians 3:28. This is because he couldn't anticipate the present wrangling over the verse, as, generally speaking, the present-day egalitarian interpretation of Galatians 3:28 is a modern phenomenon. E. de Witt Burton, *A Critical and Exegetical Commentary on the Epistle to the Galatians*, International Critical Commentary Series (Edinburgh: T. & T. Clark, 1921). On this point see S. Lewis Johnson, "Role Distinctions in the Church," in *Recovering Biblical Manhood and Womanhood*, eds. John Piper and Wayne Grudem (Wheaton, Ill.: Crossway, 1991), 155-156; and Yarbrough, "Hermeneutics," 179, note 116. This is not to deny that Galatians 3:28 was referenced in past controversies over women's suffrage or slavery. On this point see Susie C. Stanley, "Response," in *Women, Authority, and the Bible*, ed. Alvera Mickelsen (Downers Grove, Ill.: InterVarsity, 1986), 183-188. Yarbrough's comment seems to pertain to technical NT studies.

[27] Burton, *Galatians*, 206-207, italics mine. Burton raises issues that were important in his time— the merging of nationalities and the abolition of slavery. It is interesting that he didn't feel the need to address misuses of the final couplet, "there is no male or female." If he were writing today, he would surely have dealt with this issue.

[28] Ronald Y. K. Fung, "Ministry in the New Testament," in *The Church and the Bible and the World*, ed. D. A. Carson (Grand Rapids, Mich.: Baker, 1987), 183-184.

Complementarians disagree with egalitarian claims such as, "Galatians 3:28 is the most socially explosive statement in the New Testament,"[29] since, given the flow of Galatians 3–4, Paul had no intent of writing a "Magna Carta of Humanity."[30] Complementarians agree with egalitarians that there are social implications for Galatians 3:28, but they have a different conception of what these social changes might look like. Fung notes:

> It appears that the three categories [couplets] differ in nature, and that accordingly the social implementations for them are not the same. Whereas slavery, as a social institution created by sinful men, can and should be abolished, and the Jew/Gentile distinction, which retains its validity as a purely ethnic reality, has been transcended through the reconciliation accomplished by Christ (Eph. 2:14-16), the male/female distinction, unlike the other two, has its roots in creation itself and continues to have significance in the realm of redemption.[31]

So even when complementarians and egalitarians find common ground, agreeing that there are sociological implications for Galatians 3:28, they disagree upon the extent of those implications.

Finally, complementarians believe that the pivotal phrase "you are all one in Christ Jesus" emphasizes *unity* in Christ, while egalitarians see this unity as the ground for *equality*. Complementarians affirm that men and women both share in Christ, and that, as a result, both inherit the promised blessings and become children of God. But it is a mistake, they argue, to insist that equality in some respects means equality in *all* respects.[32] Complementarians are quick to point out that even *if* egalitarians are right when they insist that "you are all one in Christ" means "you are all equal in Christ," it still does not follow that men and women have the same roles, because the New Testament does not assume "that equality in the sight of God implies . . . role interchangeability among all Christians."[33]

In summary, complementarians do not believe that Galatians 3:28

[29] Snodgrass, "Galatians 3:28," 161.
[30] Paul K. Jewett, *Man as Male and Female* (Grand Rapids, Mich.: Eerdmans, 1975), 142.
[31] Fung, "Ministry in the New Testament," 184.
[32] Davis, "Some Reflections on Galatians 3:28," 204.
[33] Ibid., 203.

has much to say about the roles of men and women. The verse has much to say about the worth and status of all types of people, men and women alike, who are in Christ, but it was never written to delineate roles or functions of these groups of people. To use it for this end is to misrepresent Paul.

Using the complementarian and egalitarian positions as points of reference, I will now offer an interpretation of Galatians 3:28. I will put forth and defend four particular statements about the meaning and significance of Galatians 3:28.

## GALATIANS 3:28 DESCRIBES THE NEW PEOPLE OF GOD

Complementarians tend to ignore the salvation-historical implications of Galatians 3–4. Snodgrass is right when he states, "Whatever else is done with the other texts concerning women, justice must be done to the newness proclaimed in Galatians 3:28."[34] Although the term *new* is found nowhere in Galatians 3:26-29, these verses are preceded by 3:23-25 ("Before this faith came. . . . Now that faith has come. . . ."), and followed by 4:1-7 (". . . But when the time had fully come, God sent his Son. . . . So you are no longer a slave, but a son. . . ."); any interpretation of Galatians 3:28 must address the question, "What is new?" If the meaning of Galatians 3:28 is simply that Jews/Greeks, slaves/free, men/women all are God's people, it is difficult to see how such an interpretation does justice to the new era brought about by the arrival of Christ.

What, then, is new about the people of God in the new covenant? It is beyond the scope of this study to attempt a description of everything that is new, but it will suffice to mention two major changes that are illustrative of the type of changes resulting from the truths taught in Galatians 3:26-29.[35]

---

[34] Snodgrass, "Galatians 3:28," 178.
[35] Some have argued that the old covenant was a period of inequality and injustice for some, such as women, slaves, and Gentiles, and that the new covenant brought about equality for all. This, however, does not appear to be the distinction Paul himself draws between the old and the new (more on this in the next chapter). Often this claim is substantiated by an appeal to particular Rabbinic texts that are disparaging of women. There are, however, some Rabbinic texts that speak quite positively of women. I cite four such texts here, found in *Rabbinic Anthology*, translated by Claude G. Montefiore and H. Loewe (Cleveland, Ohio: World Publishing Co., 1963). The first two passages are from *Sifre Numbers*:
    1. "When the daughters of Zelophehad (Num. xxvii, 1-12) heard that the land was being divided among men to the exclusion of women, they assembled together to take counsel. They said: 'The com-

First, there was a corporate flavor to salvation under the law-covenant. W. D. Davies comments, "The religion of the Torah was essentially a national religion. To accept the Torah meant not merely initiation into a religion . . . but incorporation into a nation."[36] Generally speaking, since it was necessary to be tied to Abraham to inherit the promised blessings, and since Abraham was intricately linked to the Jewish nation, then naturally salvation became associated with the Jewish nation.[37]

---

*passion of God is not as the compassion of men. The compassion of men extends to men more than women, but not thus is the compassion of God; His compassion extends equally to men and women* and to all, even as it is said, "The Lord is good to all, and His mercies are over all his works"" (italics mine). *Sifre Numbers*, Pinehas, §133, f. 49a, quoted in Montefiore and Loewe, *Rabbinic Anthology*, 510.

2. "The daughters of Zelophehad said to Moses: 'Give unto us a possession among the brethren of our father' (Num. xxvii, 4). R. Nathan [A.D. 140-165] said: *'The strength [of the faith] of the women was, therefore, finer than that of the men.* For the men had said: 'Let us make a captain, and let us return to Egypt'" (italics mine). *Sifre Num.*, Pinehas, §133, f. 49b, quoted in Montefiore and Loewe, *Rabbinic Anthology*, 510.

3. "If a poor man comes, and pleads before another, that other does not listen to him; if a rich man comes, he listens to, and receives, him at once: God does not act thus: *all are equal before Him, women, slaves, rich and poor*" (italics mine). R. Judah b. Shalom [fourth century A.D.] quoted in *Exodus Rabbah* 21.4 , quoted in Montefiore and Loewe, *Rabbinic Anthology*, 346.

4. This passage is remarkably similar to Galatians 3:28: "God says to Moses, 'Is there respect of persons with me? *Whether it be Israelite or Gentile, man or woman, slave or handmaid, whoever does a good deed, shall find the reward at its side,* as it says, 'Thy righteousness is like the everlasting hills: man and beast alike thou savest, O Lord'" (italics mine). *Yalkut*, Lek leka, §76, quoted in Montefiore and Loewe, *Rabbinic Anthology*, 380.

Raphael Loewe, commenting on the role of women in Judaism, surmises, "In view of the . . . [different expectations of roles for Jewish women and men], it would be surprising if wives thought of themselves as 'equals' of their husbands, or vice versa; yet this language may give an incorrect impression of condescension on the husband's side. It might be more true to speak of a markedly recognized consciousness of the difference of *function* of the two partners to a marriage by each one of them, and to conclude that this consciousness might, but need not necessarily, lead to a feeling of their disparity." Raphael Loewe, *The Position of Women in Judaism* (London: SPCK, 1966), 23. Doubtless many Jewish men, as other men throughout the ages, have erroneously considered themselves better than women. There is no shortage of "anti-women" statements in the Rabbinic literature and other literature of the time. But Loewe, unlike many scholars, argues that Judaism did not inherently place a higher value on the role of men. Rather, Judaism viewed the role of women as being *different,* though not necessarily inferior, to that of men. "In a word, while much of the practical features of Torah and the Jewish law constitute machinery by which the Jewish ideal of 'Holiness' (*qedushah*) can be spelled out for men, Judaism acknowledges—with respect, gratitude, and due esteem—the circumstance that women possess, and can act upon an appreciation of 'Holiness' *which is no whit inferior to that of men,* but which is one that operates intuitively" (italics mine). Ibid., 50.

In summary, though far from being comprehensive and admittedly insufficient to make my case decisively, the purpose of this note is simply to question the commonly accepted paradigm that women were second-class, unjustly oppressed people in the Rabbinic writings (and some argue, by implication, the OT) and that now, in the new era of the NT, women are finally accorded justice, that is, the same roles as men. Such a position can be argued, citing various chauvinistic Rabbinic sources, but it does not appear that all the Rabbinic data fit this paradigm, and it is even more questionable if the OT, as a whole, can be portrayed as anti-women. More work needs to be done on this. On the possibility of Rabbinic sources influencing Galatians 3:28 see Madeleine Boucher, "Some Unexplored Parallels to 1 Cor 11,11-12 and Gal 3,28: The NT on the Role of Women," *Catholic Biblical Quarterly* 31 (1969): 50-58.

[36] W. D. Davies, *Paul and Rabbinic Judaism* (London: SPCK, 1962), 67.

[37] There are exceptions to the nationalistic flavor of salvation in the OT, such as the Ninevites, who repented after hearing Jonah's preaching. It is probably more precise, then, to say there was a "corporate" or "tribal" flavor to salvation under the law-covenant.

Raphael Loewe writes, "Judaism, although it may admit occasional proselytes, possesses, in Jewry, its own ethnological dimension; it is a natural community of those closely or more distantly akin, together with a minority of others whom the majority can absorb socially."[38] With the arrival of Christ and the new covenant this nationalistic/ethnological emphasis has vanished:

> Christ was . . . a revelation of God apart from the Law. This meant one could be a Christian without being a Jew, and so the doors were open to the Gentiles. In Judaism all had to be Jews, there could be no Greek nor Scythian. In Christ there could be both Jew and Greek and Scythian, the national principle had been transcended.[39]

The passing of the "national principle" opened the door to all individuals, regardless of national affiliation.[40] In the old system one outside of Judaism and the Jewish nation could feel excluded, but now, as Galatians 3:28 clearly proclaims, this is no longer true. All people can come to Christ. "The locus of the people of God is no longer national and tribal; it is international, transracial, transcultural,"[41] for there is no longer Jew/Greek, slave/free, male/female, for all are one in Christ.

Second, the new era brings a time when God's Spirit is poured out on all believers. The Spirit in the Old Testament was primarily poured out upon individuals with distinctive roles—prophets, priests, and kings. These leaders guided the nation, teaching, leading, and protecting the people. They represented God to the people, and their Spirit-empowered roles were primarily mediatorial. But though the prophets "tended to focus on the corporate results, the restoration of the nation; . . . they also anticipated a transformation of individual 'hearts'—no longer hearts of

---

[38] Loewe, *The Position of Women in Judaism*, 50.
[39] Davies, *Paul and Rabbinic Judaism*, 67.
[40] The national affiliation found in the OT is evidenced by the development of the remnant theme. The prophets warned that simply being connected to God's nation wasn't pleasing to God. God wanted individual people whose hearts were fully his. "The remnant of OT prophecy merges into the new people of God, constituted on the basis of faith in Christ. The remnant of Israel is not eliminated; but it stands alongside those Gentiles who are called to be members of God's new people." W. Günther and J. Krienke, "Remnant," in *The New International Dictionary of the New Testament*, ed. Colin Brown (Grand Rapids, Mich.: Zondervan, 1971), 3:252. Though there was a nationalistic emphasis in the OT, in the history of redemption it was gradually fulfilled in a new community consisting of individuals filled with God's Spirit, regardless of their national affiliation. Ibid.
[41] D. A. Carson, *The Gagging of God: Christianity Confronts Pluralism* (Grand Rapids, Mich.: Zondervan, 1996), 254.

stone but hearts that hunger to do God's will."[42] They looked forward
to the new, when God promised that He would "pour out [his] Spirit on
all people" (Joel 2:28) and would give each of his people a "new heart"
and a "new spirit" to follow his decrees (Ezek. 36:24-27). Galatians
3:26-29 highlights the fact that *all* God's people now are sons, and
hence, heirs. Each believer is an heir, and, as a result, each receives the
promised Spirit (Gal. 3:14; 4:6-7). God's people no longer look to specific mediatorial leaders, empowered by the Spirit to show them God's
ways. Now *all* God's people have the promised inheritance, his Spirit.

Galatians 3:28 definitely describes a new, important, and exciting
change. It is not difficult to imagine Paul's enthusiasm as he proclaimed
the truths in Galatians 3:26-29: You are *all* sons of God, you have *all*
put on Christ, you are *all* fully heirs, you *all* have God's Spirit and call
out *Abba*, Father. The new age has brought about an era where God's
Spirit indwells each believer, and each of God's people may know and
respond to him personally. It is a new time, a time of *Abba*, Father, when
God himself dwells with each of his people (cf. Ezek. 37:26-27).

In summary, it is important to recognize the "newness" of the
proclamation of Galatians 3:26-29. Complementarians and egalitarians
differ regarding the specifics of what is new, but any responsible interpretation of Galatians 3:28 must acknowledge the arrival of the new
covenant and the accompanying changes in the people of God. More
will be said below concerning possible role changes in Jews, Greeks,
slaves, free, men, and women resulting from the arrival of the new era.

## "ONENESS" IN GALATIANS 3:28 DOES NOT IMPLY UNQUALIFIED "EQUALITY"

Egalitarians have misinterpreted the phrase "you are all one in Christ."
To say that a plurality of groups of people are "one" does not mean that
the groups are "equal" to each other. Furthermore, simply because
Galatians 3:28 teaches some notion of equality, it does not follow that
it prescribes equality in an unqualified sense. To label two groups, who
are equal in one respect, "equal" is to invite confusion and
misunderstanding.

The importance of the phrase "for you are all one in Christ Jesus"

---

[42] D. A. Carson, *The Gospel According to John* (Grand Rapids, Mich.: Eerdmans, 1991), 195.

has already been noted. The reason Paul writes the negation "there is no Jew/Greek, slave/free, male/female" is *because* all of the people in these groups are one in Christ. What does Paul mean when he calls a plurality one? What is the meaning of this "oneness"?

As noted in the previous chapter, there are two critical reasons why "you are all one" does not mean "you are all equal." I will review these two reasons briefly. The first reason is the lexical range of the word *one*.[43] Lexically this word cannot mean "equal." Our overview of BAGD confirmed this, as we found that there is no known example of *one* being used this way.

The second reason "you are all one" does not mean "you are all equal" is that the phrase was not used in that way in the era of the New Testament. As we have seen, a study of every parallel use of the phrase "we/you/they are one" in the 300 years surrounding the New Testament reveals that this expression fails to express the concept of unqualified equality. In fact, "you are all one" is used of *diverse* objects to denote one element they share in common; it is not used of similar objects to denote that they are the same. It will be helpful to review some of the specific examples from the previous chapter. In 1 Corinthians 3:8 Paul writes that the one who waters and the one who plants are one. Both of these individuals have different roles and different rewards, but Paul uses the expression "you are one" to show that they share one thing in common—that they have a common purpose. In Romans 12:5 Paul writes that, "We who are many form one body, and each member belongs to all the others. We have different gifts. . . ." Again, the expression "we are one" is an expression that denotes what different people, with different gifts, have in common—one body in Christ. The pattern is the same with the Father and Son (John 10:30) and the husband and wife (Mark 10:8). In both cases the expression "you are one" highlights an element that diverse objects share in common. In the case of the Godhead, the Father and the Son, though different in person and role, share the same nature. In marriage, the husband and wife, though different in creation, in their fallenness, and in their roles,[44] share one flesh.

---

[43] Gk. εἷς
[44] When I say that husbands and wives are different in their roles, I am simply noting that, taken at face value, the NT gives husbands and wives different roles (cf. Eph. 5; Col. 3; Titus 2; 1 Pet. 3).

An author will often clarify the meaning of "you are all one" by specifically stating in what way these diverse objects are one. For example, Philo writes that Simeon and Levi are one in will. If Philo simply wrote, "Simeon and Levi are one," a reader would be left wondering "one *what*?" Because Simeon and Levi are different people, it is not inherently clear in what manner they are one. Similarly, if someone today made the statement, "The Republicans and Democrats are one," the hearer would doubtless be confused: In what sense are Republicans and Democrats one? A more likely statement would be, "Republicans and Democrats are one in their resolve to win the war on drugs." The expression, then, highlights what the diverse groups have in common; it says little or nothing about how they differ. For example, the statement, "I and the Father are one" tells us little about Christ, the Father, their roles, or their differences; all the reader knows is that they are one in some respect.

In summary, then, the lexical evidence for the word *one* as well as the usage of the phrase "you are all one" during the New Testament era are decidedly against any interpretation that tries to read unconstrained "equality" into this expression. When Paul states that Jews/Greeks, slave/free, male/female are one, he is saying that these widely diverse people share something in common. The expression "you are one" does not mean "you have so much in common," but the opposite.

The expression "you are all one" does, however, contain some notion of equality. If, for example, two objects share in R, they are equal in that they both share in R. So, if Jew/Greek, slave/free, male/female share in Christ, then they are equal in this regard—they all share in Christ. In this sense egalitarians are correct when they assert that "men and women are equal in Christ." But simply because x and y share something in common—just because they are equal in this one respect—it does not follow that x and y are equal (i.e., the same) in other respects. It is important at this point to take a brief look at the concept of *equality*.

---

Even if one argues that these roles were the result of Paul's accommodating the church to the demands of culture, and hence are no longer valid, at the time Mark 10:8 and Matthew 19:6 were written (with their expressions about marriage where a plurality is called "one") the husband and the wife would have been perceived as having different, non-interchangeable roles.

## Excursus: The Nature of Equality

The concept of equality has become central in the debate over Galatians 3:28, even though Paul never uses the *equal* word group[45] in this verse.[46] The notion of *equality*, then, is derived from the concepts and words expressed in the verse. Though this thesis has focused on the exegetical and contextual details of Galatians 3:28, it is nevertheless important to say something about the link between Galatians 3:28 and the notion of equality, for virtually every egalitarian treatment of this verse ties Galatians 3:28 to equality. James Crouch, for example, writes, "Taken at face value such a statement [Gal. 3:28] can only mean *complete equality* in the church."[47]

---

[45] Gk. ἴσος

[46] Complementarians occasionally note that Paul could have used an ἴσος ("equal") term had he desired. See, for example, Ann Coble, "The Lexical Horizon of 'One in Christ': The Use of Galatians 3:28 in the Progressive-Historical Debate over Women's Ordination," Th.M. thesis, Covenant Theological Seminary, 1995. Arguments that are built upon what the author did *not* write, but *could* have written, generally fail to make a compelling case. There is, however, a passage in Philo that uses ἴσος ("equal") in precisely the manner in which one might expect Paul would have used it had he wanted to emphasize equality. Philo, writing at about the same time as Paul, uses the phrase πάντες ἐστὲ ἰσότιμοι ("you are all entitled to equal honor"), which is almost directly parallel to Galatians 3:28 πάντες εἷς ἐστέ ("you are all one"). Philo, *de Vita Mosis* [*On the Life of Moses*] 1:324 : "Ye are all entitled to equal honour, ye are one race, ye have the same fathers, one house, ye have the same customs . . . every one of which binds your kindred closer together and cements your mutual good will; why then when you are thought worthy of equal shares of the most important and most necessary things, do you show a covetous spirit in the division of the lands . . .?" (trans. C. D. Yonge). This passage addresses a situation where two of the tribes tried to settle prematurely in their allotment of land, leaving the other ten tribes to fight the upcoming battles. They were rebuked: "Shall you then sit here and enjoy leisure . . . [while] the most extreme dangers await others?" (322). Moses reminded them that "It is for the sake of the whole that the parts are thought worthy of any inheritance at all." It is because God set his favor and promises on Israel as a whole that any of the tribes had an inheritance. And since each tribe had equal honor, there should be no "covetous spirit" or preferential treatment between the tribes. Note: i) Philo uses an ἴσος root word, but translators qualify it: "Ye are all entitled to equal *honour*." The twelve tribes weren't equal in many ways, but they were deserving of equal honor. The Loeb Classical Series translates this, "You have all equal rights with us." ii) Moses' argument here is much like Galatians 3:28. The parts (Jew/Greek, slave/free, male/female) have inheritance only because of the whole (being in Christ). If, then, the tribes are united in the most important issue (being a nation) Moses argues there should be no division or "covetous spirits" between the parts. iii) Some might see this passage as evidence for the egalitarian position: On the basis of the promises given to the nation as a whole, each part has equal honor; thus, each part should be treated in the same manner. But notice, while each tribe has equal *honor*, and each is treated the same way when it comes to fighting battles or settling land, not all the tribes have the same roles (e.g., Gen. 49:10, "the scepter will not depart from Judah," and Numbers 3, which details the unique role of the tribe of Levi). Surely all the tribes are equal—in one sense—and surely, as a result of this joint heritage they should work together to do good to one another. But the inheritance, which belongs to each tribe as a result of being part of a whole, does not negate the uniqueness of each tribe. Thus, even if Paul had used an ἴσος ("equal") word in Galatians 3:28, it would not follow that Jew/Greek, slave/free, male/female have the same roles. In addition, the fact that Paul did *not* use an ἴσος root word, when it was available, is evidence, though admittedly not weighty, that his intent was not to emphasize the equality of Jew/Greek, slave/free, male/female.

[47] James E. Crouch, *The Origin and Intention of the Colossian Haustafel* (Göttingen, Germany: Vandenhoeck & Ruprecht, 1972), 141, italics mine.

What does it mean for two entities to be equal? If a seven-year-old, for example, asks his father, "Does a cup of sugar equal a cup of flour?" the father faces a dilemma. If the son's question means, "Is a cup of one granular material the same volume as a cup of another granular material?" the answer is yes. If, on the other hand, he is asking, "Can I put a cup of sugar in this recipe for a cup of flour, since they are equal?" the answer is no. A cup of sugar and a cup of flour are equal in one respect, but not in all respects. The statement, "A cup of sugar and a cup of flour are equal," is valid and true, provided one understands the manner in which the two entities are equal.

Consider the Declaration of Independence. It states, "We hold these truths to be self-evident, that all men are created equal." This statement is both true and false, depending on what one means by "equal." Surely there are many ways in which all people are *not* equal: All people do not write like Shakespeare or jump like Michael Jordan; all people are not given the same educational or vocational opportunities; and people are certainly given different starts in life due to their family situations. But the writers of the Declaration did believe that all people do have certain unalienable, God-given rights. So, to avoid confusion, they clarified what they intended by the term *equal* with a series of dependent clauses: "that they are endowed by their Creator with certain unalienable Rights, that among these are Life, Liberty, and the pursuit of Happiness." "All men are created equal" is a profound statement, provided one rightly understands what is intended by "equal."

Both of these examples show that the claim "x and y are equal" really means "x and y are equal in some defined respect." This is true not only in modern examples; the New Testament period also contains examples of this. Consider Philo, *Quis Her.* ["Who Is the Heir"] 164:

> It is equality [God] also that divided the human race into man and woman, making two divisions, *unequal* in strength, but most perfectly *equal* for the purpose which nature had principally in view, the generation of a third human being like themselves. For, says Moses, "God made man; in the image of God created he him; male and female he created them." He no longer says "him," but "them," in the plural number . . . .[48]

---

[48] *The Works of Philo*, new updated edition, trans. C. D. Yonge (Peabody, Mass.: Hendrickson, 1993), 289, italics mine.

In this passage Philo calls men and women unequal in one regard but equal in another. Elsewhere, in *Quis Her.* 133-161, Philo has a lengthy discourse on equality, citing many different uses of the term *equal*: equal numbers (2 + 2 = 4), equal magnitudes (equal weights or capacities), and equal proportions (e.g., when each citizen is ordered to make an equal contribution from his property, the contributions are not, of course, numerically equal, but equal in the sense that it is proportionate to the valuation of each citizen's estate). Philo even notes that the smallest animals are proportionally equal to the largest—e.g., the mullet to the whale. These examples from Philo are sufficient to demonstrate that the term *equal* can be used in many different ways and consequently needs qualification. The statement, "A whale is equal to a mullet" can be true or false, depending on what is meant by "equal."

The Rabbinic literature reflects the same concept of equality. Two people or objects that are called "equal" can be in many ways quite different. As a result the authors often qualify the term *equal*. For example, in *Exodus Rabbah,* Beshallah 21.4, R. Judah b. Shalom (fourth century A.D.) says, "If a poor man comes, and pleads before another, that other does not listen to him; if a rich man comes, he listens to, and receives, him at once: God does not act thus: *all are equal before Him,* women, slaves, rich and poor."[49] Here, similarly to Galatians 3:28, two opposite groups, the rich and poor, are said to be equal *before God.* This, however, does not mean that the rich are equal to the poor in other areas, simply that they are equal before God. Here again is the pattern where "x and y are equal" means "x and y are equal in some respect(s)," not "x and y are equal in all respects."

And, as G. Stählin has shown in his article on the Greek word ἴσος ("equal"), the New Testament itself contains examples of equality/inequality that fit this pattern as well:

> Christian [*sic*] are equal on earth and in heaven. This is confirmed by the gift of the Spirit and the Word of Jesus. But there is also inequality in the community both on earth and in heaven. In addition to outward differences, e.g., between slaves and free men, rich and poor, Greeks and barbarians etc., there are also inward differences. Even in

---

[49] Montefiore and Loewe, *Rabbinic Anthology,* 346, italics mine.

gifts of grace which are granted there are essential differences (cf. Mt. 25:14ff.; 1 C. 12, esp. v. 28ff.; R. 12:6ff.; also Eph. 4:16). Even receptivity to Jesus and His Word (cf. Mk 4:24) and faith itself (cf. esp. R. 12:3: ὡς ὁ θεὸς ἐμέρισεν μέτρον πίστεως [in accordance with the measure of faith God has given you] though cf. 2 Pt. 1:1) point to different levels in individual Christians. Indeed, the NT expects distinctions in the new life. In the parable of Mt. 20:1ff. the established equality is also inequality.[50]

Whether one prefers an example from the Declaration of Independence, from Rabbinic literature, or from the Bible itself, it is clear that the expression "x and y are equal" means "x and y are equal in some respect."

Peter Westen, in his work *Speaking of Equality: An Analysis of the Rhetorical Force of 'Equality' in Moral and Legal Discourse,* provides some basic parameters that are quite helpful in considering the concept of equality: His basic definition of "descriptive equality" will help provide clarity in the discussion regarding the equality of men and women:

Descriptive equality is the relationship that obtains among two or more distinct things that have been jointly measured by a common standard and found to be indistinguishable, or identical, as measured by that standard. Things that are equal by one standard of comparison are inevitably unequal by other standards, and vice versa. It therefore follows that the things of this world that we are capable of measuring are not *either* equal *or* unequal. They are *both* equal *and* unequal.[51]

Westen points out that, in order to call two things "equal," one must at least have i) two distinct entities, ii) a means of measurement, and iii) a common standard. If the common standard (iii) in the cup of sugar/flour illustration is volume, the two cups are equal. If, on the other hand, the common standard is substance, they are unequal. Likewise, if the common standard in the Declaration of Independence is artistic ability, all people are *not* created equal. If, however, the common standard is cer-

---

[50] G. Stählin, "ἴσος," *TDNT*, 3:350-351.
[51] Peter Westen, *Speaking of Equality: An Analysis of the Rhetorical Force of 'Equality' in Moral and Legal Discourse* (Princeton, N.J.: Princeton University Press, 1990), 41, italics his.

tain rights before God, then all people *are* created equal. Westen correctly notes that it is *crucial* to clarify the common standard of comparison, for, as he says, "things that are equal by one standard of comparison are inevitably unequal by other standards."[52] Even two distinct one dollar bills are equal by one standard of comparison (worth) and unequal in other standards (age, color, etc.). Inevitably, as Westen notes, things in life are not equal *or* unequal, but both equal *and* unequal, depending upon the standard of comparison, so it is confusing at best to call two things equal without clearly delineating the standard of comparison.[53]

For example, consider the claim that two basketball players are equal. In order to determine if this is true one needs a means of measurement (ii) and a common standard (iii). Perhaps one player is a better rebounder and the other player is a better scorer; one plays better defense and the other is the strong leader of the team, especially in critical situations. How can one determine if these players are "equal"? To call them equal without an objective standard would be subjective opinion at best. One needs both a standard, such as the ability to score points, and a measurement, such as the number of points per game. It would then be possible to say that player A and player B are equal basketball players in that they both average the same number of points per game. But even if these two players average the same number of points a game, it would nevertheless be misleading to say player A and player B are equal basketball players. They are only equal given a measurable common standard of comparison. Examples like this are plentiful: What does it mean that two jobs are equal? Or that two cities are equal? Or that two graduate programs are equal? In order to determine the truthfulness of these claims one needs a means of measurement and a common standard.

Proponents of both the egalitarian and the complementarian sides, though perhaps failing to understand Westen's basic parameters, have intuitively recognized the need to qualify the term *equal*, for it is obvious to virtually everyone that men and women are not completely equal. Men and women, for example, assuredly do not have equal (i.e., the

[52] Ibid.
[53] Ibid.

same) physical traits. Thus, consider how some egalitarians have modified the term *equal:* "They [men and women] are equally *members of his body*,"[54] Paul sought to equalize "the *status* of male and female in Christ,"[55] "We err greatly if we do not insist on equal *standing* for women with men in Christ,"[56] "They still remain male and female, but such distinctions become immaterial to their equal *participation in the life of the church.*"[57]

Complementarians have likewise modified the term *equal.* Werner Neuer comments, "Galatians 3:28 means, therefore, that *as far as eternal salvation is concerned*, all, *whether male or female*, are equal before God and that each one may enjoy divine sonship through faith in Jesus (cf. Gal. 3:29)."[58] John Jefferson Davis, while acknowledging that both men and women are equally entrusted with the joint exercises of dominion and image-bearing in Genesis 1:26-28, comments that it would be erroneous to conclude "that equality in *some* respects entails equality in *all* respects."[59]

Both egalitarians and complementarians claim gender "equality" but fail to clearly specify either the means of measurement (ii) or the standard of comparison (iii). Great confusion results. Note that both groups will heartily agree with the statement, "Men and women are equal in Christ." Both groups will even gladly embrace the statement, "Men and women have equal roles in Christ."[60] In these two affirmations, however, both sides mean something substantially different. In summary, the nature of the concept of *equal* demands careful qualification—a means of measurement (ii) and a clear standard of comparison (iii).[61]

There is nothing inherently wrong with the concept of equality; properly clarified, it is a biblical concept. The crux of the issue is this:

---

[54] Boomsma, *Male and Female*, 38, italics mine.
[55] Bruce, *Galatians*, 190, italics mine.
[56] Snodgrass, "Galatians 3:28," 178, italics mine.
[57] Bilezikian, *Beyond Sex Roles*, 128, italics mine.
[58] Werner Neuer, *Man and Woman in Christian Perspective*, trans. Gordon Wenham (Wheaton, Ill.: Crossway, 1991), 108, italics mine.
[59] Davis, "Some Reflections on Galatians 3:28," 204, italics his.
[60] Complementarians will say, "Sure, men and women have equal roles—equally *valid* and equally *important*." Egalitarians will understand the statement that men and women have equal roles to mean that men and women have the *same* roles.
[61] Note: Complementarians can agree with three of the four egalitarians quoted two paragraphs above, depending on what is meant by the term "equal." They can agree that: i) men and women are equally members of Christ's body; ii) men and women have equal status in Christ, and iii) men and women have equal standing in Christ.

What is the standard of comparison when someone asserts that Galatians 3:28 teaches the equality of men and women? Equal in what sense? Equal value? Equal abilities? Equal roles? Equal callings? Equal inheritance in Christ? And how is this "equality" to be measured?

In light of what we have learned about the nature of equality, we can see that "oneness" in Galatians 3:28 does not imply unqualified equality. While the expression "you are all one" doubtless implies some notion of equality for Jew/Gentile, slave/free, man/woman, it does not follow that men and women are equal in all regards. The lexical data will not allow this, nor does the expression "you are all one" mean this. And simply because "you are all one" implies some notion of equality,[62] it does not follow that men and women are equal in an unqualified sense. Any meaningful statement on the relationship between *equality* and Galatians 3:28 must clearly state a common standard of comparison. Hence, unqualified statements such as "Galatians 3:28 teaches the equality of men and women" are both dangerously imprecise and potentially misleading.

## GALATIANS 3:28 DOES NOT PRIMARILY ADDRESS THE ISSUE OF SEXUAL ROLES

While rightly pointing to the need to consider the social implications of Galatians 3:28, egalitarians are mistaken when they consider the "primary" focus of this verse as being horizontal relationships within the

---

[62] Gilbert Bilezikian believes that the concept of *oneness* requires equal (i.e., the same) status and roles. Any form of authority is, according to Bilezikian, counter to oneness. He is cited in *World* magazine as saying, "There cannot be authentic community as described in the New Testament without the full inclusion of the constituency of members into the ministry, life, and leadership of the group." Susan Olasky, "The Feminist Seduction of the Evangelical Church: Femme Fatale, *World*, March 29, 1997, 14. In other words, male headship, either in the home or in the church, is precluded by the notion of oneness. Thus, the "oneness" of Galatians 3:28 *requires* sameness in role. Bilezikian takes this a step further when he applies this principle to the Trinity. In a recent article in *JETS* he writes, "Eternal subordination [of the Son to the Father] precludes equality." Gilbert Bilezikian, "Hermeneutical Bungee-Jumping: Subordination in the Godhead," *Journal of the Evangelical Theological Society* 40 (1997): 64. In other words, because the Father and Son are one, there cannot be subordination in the Godhead.

Other egalitarians, such as Klyne Snodgrass, see no *a priori* conflict between headship and equality. Bilezikian's claim that any authority violates equality or oneness is, it seems to me, counter to both common experience and the biblical evidence. For a brief defense of headship within the Trinity see Stephen D. Kovach, "Egalitarians Revamp Doctrine of the Trinity: Bilezikian, Grenz and the Kroegers Deny Eternal Subordination of the Son," *CBMW News*, vol. 2, no. 1 (December 1996): 1-5.

Christian community.[63] To be fair, most egalitarians rightly say that the primary focus of 3:28 is theological and the social implications are only secondary. Anyone who has extensively read egalitarian studies on Galatians 3:28, however, will readily notice that the ostensibly "secondary" becomes the primary. The very reason Galatians 3:28 has become a lightning rod in the contemporary debate over the roles of men and women is that egalitarians have trumpeted this verse as teaching that men and women have interchangeable roles in the home and church. Does Galatians 3:28 address the question of the roles of men and women? There are three contextual and structural considerations that reveal that Paul's primary concern was *not* with the roles of each of these groups.

### The Flow of Paul's Argument

First, the entire flow of Paul's argument from 2:15 through 3:29 and beyond is salvation-historical. He is concerned with issues such as the purpose and relevance of the law, the fulfillment of the promise, and the changes brought about by the arrival of Christ. The major story line is the progression from Abraham and the heirs-to-be of the promise made to him, to the fulfillment of this promise in Christ and the consequent blessing of all who are in him. The concepts of the *one* and the *many* are critical in this regard. The many (the heirs-to-be) were in the one (Abraham). He was their representative head, and the blessings of the promise came only through him, the one. In the same way Christ is the one Seed; only through him can the promised inheritance be received. The many are blessed through their relationship to the one.

When the flow of Galatians 3–4 is considered, it is evident that Paul's concern was not with how the *many* relate to *one another* or behave in the church or home. His main emphasis was that the *many*, because of their tie to the *one* (to Christ), are now heirs of the blessings promised to Abraham. All individuals, regardless of their tribal or family connection, financial condition, or sex, are heirs of the promise.

It is significant that neither the starting point nor what follows in Paul's argument is concerned with the role relationships of these different groups. Some may argue that 2:11-14 shows that the starting point

---

[63] Boomsma, *Male and Female*, 35.

of Paul's argument was, in fact, the roles of Jews and Gentiles. This view of the Antioch problem is somewhat reductionistic, however, as the real problem for Paul was not table etiquette, but rather that Peter's behavior represented a return to the past that, in essence, denied the reality of what Christ had accomplished. That this is the case is evident by the content of Paul's argument in Galatians 2:15ff. Paul's argument in Galatians 3–4 was *theological:* What was the state of the old law-covenant now that the new covenant had arrived? His argument was theological from the beginning.

Some may argue that it is artificial to label an argument "theological" and thus deny the accompanying sociological implications. While such a dogmatic division would obviously be wrong, one should nevertheless respect the main flow and intention of an author's argument. Here in Galatians 3–4 Paul is fundamentally theological, and we should interpret him in this way. It is an error to consider his primary intent as sociological, just as it would be an error to ignore those dimensions completely.[64] Glasswell rightly says that, "To see the issue in social or cultural terms is to distort Paul's argument and leads to false applications of Paul's principles." The main issue, according to Glasswell, is the "eschatological significance of being in Christ."[65] The main issue for Paul is the universal availability of the new covenant in Christ, and one must be careful not to distort that emphasis.

### The Logic of 3:26-29

A second reason it is likely that Galatians 3:28 has little to say specifically about the roles of men and women is that 3:28 is framed by 3:26 and 3:29. These opening and closing statements reveal the heart of the paragraph 3:26-29: "You are all sons . . . then you are Abraham's seed, and heirs according to the promise." Paul's purpose is to describe how sonship, which is now available to all through God's Son, also results in one's becoming an heir of the promises to Abraham. Since i) 3:26-29 describes the fulfillment of the promise made to Abraham, and ii) the promise made to Abraham highlighted the universal nature of this inheritance—"*all* the peoples on earth will be blessed through you" (Gen.

---

[64] M. E. Glasswell, "Some Issues of Church and Society in Light of Paul's Eschatology," 310-311.
[65] Ibid., 316.

12:3)—then it is highly likely that iii) the purpose of the three negated couplets in 3:28 is to express the universality of the new people of God: *All* people can be included.

The opening and closing statements, verses 26 and 29, provide the context for verse 28. If Paul's purpose is to teach about the universal availability of the inheritance, it is difficult to understand how the respective roles of Jew/Greek, slave/free, male/female fit into his argument. No doubt there may be implications for the roles of men and women, but the structure of the passage clearly shows that Paul's intended emphasis was the universal nature of the new inheritance, not the respective roles of those who receive it.

*The Implications of "You Are All One"*

A third reason that Paul likely did not have of roles in mind in Galatians 3:28 stems from the critical expression "you are all one." As we have seen, this expression is used to show what *diverse* objects have in common. It does not address how these objects differ or function. If Paul's intent had been to show that men and women have the *same* roles—that their roles are interchangeable in many ways—it is doubtful that he would have used this expression. The expression "you are all one," while pointing to a shared element, nevertheless *assumes differences* between the individual entities. The New Testament examples of "we/you/they are one," where a plurality of people are called one, are: the planter and waterer (1 Cor. 3:8); Father and Son (John 10:30; 17:11, 21, 22 [2x], 23); husband and wife (Matt. 19:6; Mark 10:8); and different believers with different gifts (Rom. 12:5; 1 Cor. 10:17). *In every instance the groups of people in these pairs have different roles.* Given these expressions, which formally are directly parallel with Galatians 3:28, it is difficult to see how the meaning of "you are all one" can be "there are no distinctions of role between you."

Is it not possible, then, that even though Paul's intent was not to address the roles of men and women *directly,* there are still some important *implications* of the truth of Galatians 3:28 for men's and women's roles? This seems more in line with Paul's thought.

The advent of the new as described in Galatians 3:28 inevitably means changes in the roles of Jews/Greeks, slaves/free, male/female. Masters are told to treat their slaves well, and slaves are told to obey their masters with sincerity of heart (Eph. 6:5ff.). Although this concept wasn't totally new—the Old Testament had provisions to protect slaves (Ex. 21:2; Lev. 25:47-55)[66]—these roles are now different because both masters and slaves are one in Christ. Similarly, Jews could no longer gloat over their national identity to the exclusion of the Gentiles (Rom. 2:17ff.). God's people, now Jew and Gentile, should relate to one another in a new way (Eph. 2:14ff.) because they are both now one in Christ. And, in the new era the husband is told to love his wife as his own body and to offer himself up for her as Christ offered himself for the church; and the wife is told to submit to her husband and respect him (Eph. 5:22ff.). Again, although this teaching is not a decisive break from the Old Testament,[67] the new era does bring about something new.

In summary, it would be foolish to insist that the roles of these six groups did not change when the "fullness of time" arrived. Paul is fully aware that, since all believers are now "in Christ," relationships between them will be transformed. This is implied by Galatians 3:28 and confirmed by the rest of Paul's writings. The acknowledgment of this reality, however, is a far cry from the egalitarian position that Galatians 3:28 is the most socially explosive statement in the New Testament. This verse cannot be the most socially explosive statement in the New Testament because Paul's primary intent was not sociological. The flow of Galatians 3–4 confirms this, as does the structure of Galatians 3:26-29 and the implications of the expression "you are all one." Ward Gasque is mistaken when he writes, "[Paul] is focusing on the new social reality created by our baptism into Christ."[68] Paul is *not* focusing on the new social reality, which is precisely why a fair interpretation of Galatians 3:28 must not make social roles the primary focus of this verse. As Köstenberger aptly summarizes:

> Of course, some insist Paul's statements in Gal 3:28 *imply* a change in human relationships. But whether a change in human relationship is

---

[66] Grant Osborne, *The Hermeneutical Spiral: A Comprehensive Introduction to Biblical Interpretation* (Downers Grove, Ill.: InterVarsity, 1991), 12.

[67] The OT speaks highly of the godly wife (Gen. 1:26-27; Prov. 12:4; Prov. 31) and encourages the husband to be committed to his wife (Gen. 2:24; Mal. 2:14ff.). In the OT God himself is said to be a "husband" to his people (Jer. 31:32), indicating that the OT concept of "husband" did not have demeaning implications.

[68] W. Ward Gasque, "Response" in *Women, Authority, and the Bible*, ed. Alvera Mickelsen (Downers Grove, Ill.: InterVarsity, 1986), 189.

implied in Gal 3:28 or not, this does not appear to be the point Paul actually intended to make. The interpreter should take care to distinguish between authorial intention and possible implications. Moreover, it seems questionable to focus on the implications of Paul's statements to the extent that the point Paul actually intended to make all but retreats into the background.[69]

There is great danger in focusing on possible implications of a passage to the exclusion of its central intent.

Those who see the primary focus of Galatians 3:28 as gender roles in the family and church misapply this Scripture. Even though rightly insisting on changes in God's people in the new era, they specify these changes by speculatively reading role relations into a passage that does not directly address roles. Galatians 3:28 then is viewed as the pinnacle of biblical teaching on the roles of men and women. The new age did bring about sociological and relational changes, at least in some respects, but these changes should be defined by passages that directly address this issue.

## GALATIANS 3:28 HAS SOCIAL IMPLICATIONS

Complementarians, in general, minimalize the social implications of Galatians 3:28. If men and women are one in Christ, what are some of the implications for Christian families, churches, and organizations? How can God's people daily reflect their oneness in Christ?

We must proceed carefully when seeking to derive specific social applications from the theological truths contained in Galatians 3:28, as societal roles were not Paul's primary focus in the passage. Nevertheless, the principles Paul has provided do have behavioral ramifications. Three principles, which can guide specific applications, seem clear from the text. First, all God's people are in Christ. Second, all God's people, by virtue of being in Christ, are one. Third, the great mercies and blessings of God are given to all God's people, without distinction, regardless of one's sex, race, or social/financial background.

Although many applications could be drawn from these three prin-

---

[69] Andreas Köstenberger, "Gender Passages in the NT: Hermeneutical Fallacies Critiqued." *Westminster Theological Journal* 56 (1994), 277.

ciples, the following applications seem both fair to the text and pertinent for our culture and church today.

   i) Since all God's people share in Christ, there is no room for boast-
ing or comparison for any reason, but certainly not on the basis of race,
gender, or social standing. Feelings of superiority, as well as feelings of
inferiority, both stem from an erroneous view of God's people in the new
age. Under the old law-covenant, "The Jews' superiority over the
Gentiles consisted in the fact that they believed themselves to be direct
lineal descendants of the Patriarchs. This direct lineal descent was very
important, for it guaranteed the benefits of God's election and love and
was the assurance of final salvation. For the Jews the phrase 'seed of
Abraham' was not a metaphor but a biological fact."[70] This kind of
"superiority" or privilege has no place in the new era. If these attitudes
exist in a body of God's people, they should be rooted out by the truth
that *all* God's people share in the same Christ. Each believer should
search his or her own heart, seeking to rectify any thoughts of superiority. Likewise, every person who serves as a leader among God's people should continually strive to help all under his or her care to know
and experience the truth taught in Galatians 3:28, that all God's people
are equally valuable in light of their equal relationship with Christ. Peter
O'Brien puts this well:

> In Christ there is no inferiority of the one sex to the other, or one class
> to another; men and women of completely diverse origins are gathered
> together in unity in Christ through a common allegiance to their Lord.
> There is no difference in spiritual status between them.[71]

   ii) Since God's people are one, the family of God should be characterized by unity. In Galatians 3–4, "one" is used first in the sense of
incorporation (the many in the one), and then, derivatively, for unity.
Unity is a prevalent New Testament theme (e.g., 1 Cor. 12:14ff.; Eph.
4:3ff.) as it is an important public demonstration of the reality that all

---

[70] James D. Hester, *Paul's Concept of Inheritance: A Contribution to the Understanding of
Heilsgeschichte*, Scottish Journal of Theology Occasional Papers, no. 14 (Edinburgh: Oliver and
Boyd, 1968), 52.
[71] Peter T. O'Brien, *Colossians, Philemon*, Word Biblical Commentary (Waco, Tex.: Word, 1982),
193.

believers share in one Christ. Most churches and Christian groups, however, don't have united hearts and minds. Self-centeredness, racism, and sexism all contribute to the fracturing of God's family. Galatians 3:28 implies that every effort should be made to create and maintain unity among God's diverse people. This might include regular times of fellowship where people are encouraged to take steps to reconcile with others if necessary. Another means to promote unity is to emphasize programs and structures that facilitate the development of close relationships within local churches. It is difficult to demonstrate unity without significant relationships. Each person in God's family needs to act on the truth of Galatians 3:28, seeking both to build and to preserve a united people of God.

iii) God's people are diverse, yet stand equally before him. Those who are racially, sexually, and socially different from us should be cherished and valued. There is no room for outcasts in the church, whether the discrimination be overt or subtle. All people, regardless of race, gender, or social status, are clearly members of God's family. When there are problems in this area, God's people should be proactive in seeking solutions. Programs that emphasize racial reconciliation, such as Promise Keepers, are excellent applications of the truth of Galatians 3:28. A similar project, which might be equally profitable (though I've never heard of one being implemented) could focus on gender reconciliation. Certainly there are bitter women who have not been valued or respected, and likewise, angry men. It would be good for God's people to acknowledge the different hurts and needs of men and women, and then affirm their mutual respect and need for each other because of the truth of Galatians 3:28. As society "progresses" in its radical distortion of sexual identity, there will be an even greater need for something such as this.

iv) The emphasis in Galatians 3:28 on universality, that people from all nations and walks of life comprise God's people, should challenge us to think more broadly about God's mission. As missiologists have observed, people tend to be ethnocentric: They naturally view the world through their own cultural perspective and intrinsically value what is important to them. Galatians 3:28 reveals God's universal heart for people; he is not ethnocentric, and we need to begin to think beyond our own culturally limited perspective. Those who love God the Redeemer will progressively love what he loves—people from all walks of life.

Surely other applications could be offered. The important issue, however, is to tie these applications as closely as possible to Paul's intent in the passage.

At the beginning of this chapter, I delineated four structural and contextual considerations that should serve to guide any interpretation of Galatians 3:28. I trust that the interpretation I have offered and defended fits these four guidelines:

i) The couplets are interpreted in a parallel manner, as the structure requires. The three couplets function as merisms (pairs of opposites) to describe the universal nature of the new covenant—*all* people are included. Though there are differences between the couplets, Paul uses them in a parallel fashion.

ii) The pivotal phrase "for you are all one in Christ Jesus" provides the rationale for the negation ("neither . . . nor") of the three couplets. The reason for the negations is that God's people are now known by being in Christ, not by any nationalistic or tribal affiliation. Labels such as Jew/Greek, slave/free, male/female, though important in their own right, are irrelevant when it comes to becoming heirs of the promise.

iii and iv) The interpretation offered fits the overall flow of Galatians 3–4, as well as the micro-structure of the unit of thought contained in 3:26-29. The promise to Abraham was universal. Now, in its fulfillment, it is, as predicted, universally available to all, whether Jew or Greek, slave or free, male or female.

# 4

# A Response to a Recent Egalitarian Interpretation of Galatians 3:28

In the previous chapter I have proposed and defended an interpretation of Galatians 3:28 that I believe best fits both the context of Galatians 3–4 and the exegetical specifics of 3:26-29. This final chapter will contrast my interpretation of Galatians 3:28 with the interpretation put forth by Rebecca Groothuis in her recent book *Good News for Women: A Biblical Picture of Gender Equality*.[1] Groothuis's argument for gender equality draws upon other biblical passages besides Galatians 3:28, but this verse is foundational to her case: "Of all the texts that support biblical equality, Galatians 3:26-28 is probably the most important."[2] Groothuis's work is heralded as significant by many leading egalitarian scholars. Craig Keener comments, "Relentless in its logic, yet reader-friendly, Groothuis's work is one of the best argued books on gender equality so far."[3] While it is true that Rebecca Groothuis cannot speak for all egalitarians, and that her interpretation of Galatians 3:28 is in some ways unique,[4] nevertheless her perspective on this verse has much in common with that of many other egalitarians.

---

[1] Rebecca Merrill Groothuis, *Good News for Women: A Biblical Picture of Gender Equality* (Grand Rapids, Mich.: Baker, 1997). I chose Groothuis as a representative of the egalitarian perspective because her work is well-respected and current, and because she makes extensive use of Galatians 3:28.

[2] Ibid., 25.

[3] Ibid., back cover.

[4] Rather than argue for the social implications of Galatians 3:28, as most egalitarians do, Groothuis starts from the spiritual equality taught in Galatians 3:28 and argues that the comple-

## GALATIANS 3:28 IN *GOOD NEWS FOR WOMEN*

In order to fairly summarize Groothuis's position on Galatians 3:28, I surveyed her entire book to locate every place where she refers to this verse.[5] From these many references, I compiled the following five statements that represent her use of Galatians 3:28:[6]

i) *Galatians 3:28 is the most important verse in the Bible on equality.* Virtually every reference Groothuis makes to this verse is accompanied by a statement regarding equality. For example, "Galatians 3:28 speaks of the spiritual equality and unity that all believers enjoy under the new covenant,"[7] Galatians 3:26-28 declares "the spiritual equality of all believers,"[8] "In the new covenant, all members are equal members. . . . This is what Galatians 3:26-28 is all about,"[9] "There *is* a contradiction between the essential, spiritual equality taught in Galatians 3:26-28 and the universal principle of female subordination to male spiritual authority that traditionalists believe is taught else-

---

mentarian position is internally incoherent because the roles that complementarians require of men and women contradict the spiritual equality taught in 3:28.

[5] Galatians 3:28 is mentioned (in *Good News for Women*) on pages 20, 25, 26 (2x), 27 (3x), 28 (2x), 29, 30, 31, 34, 35 (2x), 36 (4x), 37 (3x), 38 (2x), 39 (2x), 41, 100, 106, 111, 181, 189, 193, and 232. I trust that this list is exhaustive. In an effort to represent fairly Groothuis's position I asked for her feedback on this synthesis of her views. Her input was quite helpful, as I had inadvertently misconstrued portions of her position in my first draft. While this is the corrected version, it is, of course, still *my* synthesis of her position; I hope that it is fair and accurate. I am grateful that she took the time to respond to my work in such a thorough manner.

[6] Groothuis uses different terms than I use for the complementarian position. I will use her terms to present her argument. She rejects the label "complementarian" because she believes that it is "ambiguous" (p. 15): "Discussion of gender roles is so easily obfuscated, overheated, and sidetracked, it is important that our terminology be as precise as possible. Unlike the other terms for the nonegalitarian position, 'complementarian' does not point to the distinctive beliefs that are at issue in this debate. It could just as easily be used to describe a position of biblical equality; certainly no one is claiming that men and women do not complement one another" (p. 15). Groothuis herself believes that men and women complement each other; so instead of "complementarian" she opts for terms such as "traditionalist," "advocates of gender hierarchy," "gender role traditionalists," and "hierarchalist," to name a few. These terms, she believes, better point to the distinctive differences in the positions.

It should be noted, however, that some complementarians have disavowed the labels "traditionalist" and "hierarchalist," stating that these terms *fail* to characterize their position (for example, see John Piper and Wayne Grudem, eds., *Recovering Biblical Manhood and Womanhood* [Wheaton, Ill.: Crossway, 1991], xiv). Groothuis, then, uses terms to portray complementarians that some of them have disavowed. She does this because she feels that her terms better clarify the distinctive beliefs of the two positions. Admittedly no label is perfect—I, after all, could be called an egalitarian in that I believe men and women are equal as I would define "equal"—but my preference would be for her to use labels to portray an individual's position that *that individual* would use to characterize his or her own position, even if one disagrees with the accuracy of the label.

[7] Groothuis, *Good News,* 27.
[8] Ibid., 29.
[9] Ibid., 35.

where in the New Testament."[10] Many more references could be cited. A central message of Galatians 3:28, according to Groothuis, is spiritual equality.

ii) *Galatians 3:28 describes one of the theological consequences of the inauguration of the new covenant, which provides spiritual equality for all, in contrast to the old covenant, which gave privileged status almost exclusively to freeborn Jewish males:*

> The new covenant was instituted at the resurrection of Jesus Christ. God's first move after this momentous change in the spiritual order was to commission the women who had come to the empty grave with the ministry of proclaiming the Good News (the gospel) to the other believers. . . . This was God's clear refutation of the Jewish belief that women were liars and, hence, could not be trusted as witnesses. It also was an intimation of the truth of Galatians 3:26-28. The old order, in which religious life was almost exclusively in the hands of free Jewish men, had given way to a new order, in which there should no longer be any distinction in spiritual roles or privileges between Jew or Gentile, slave or free, male or female. Under the old covenant, Jesus chose free Jewish males for his apostles. Under the new covenant, women were the first to be commissioned to preach the gospel message.[11]

Groothuis clearly views Galatians 3:28 as describing an important moment in salvation-history. The new has eradicated the old system of inequality, replacing it with a new covenant of equality: "Women are now equal with men (and slaves with free persons, and Gentiles with Jews) in a way that they were not under the Old Testament Law."[12]

iii) *Galatians 3:28 not only means that men and women are joint recipients of the blessings of Christ, but that men and women have equal opportunities to participate in leadership in the home and in the religious community.* The new covenant ensures equal spiritual status and opportunity for all:

---

[10] Ibid., 37, italics hers.
[11] Ibid., 193.
[12] Ibid., 31.

In the new covenant, all members are equal members, with full privileges of membership in the spiritual body of Christ. Men and women
are not just "equally saved" (whatever that means). Rather, men and
women have equal status in the community into which their salvation
has secured their membership. All are not simply equally *in* the community of believers, but all enjoy equal opportunity to participate in
the spiritual and religious life of the community. This is what Galatians
3:26-28 is all about.[13]

Galatians 3:26-28, then, teaches that every member of God's community may participate equally in the religious life of the community,
regardless of one's gender, social class, or race. There are no "built-in
limitations of status or religious privilege"[14] simply because a person
belongs to a particular group of people:

The idea of a religious pecking order along lines of race, class, or gender is alien to the new order in Christ. Special spiritual prerogatives
no longer belong only to males (or Jews, or freeborn citizens). No particular ethnic, sexual, or social class of believers has the intrinsic right
to exercise spiritual authority over or assume spiritual responsibility
for believers outside the privileged class. All are equal members and
full participants. . . . Free Jewish male believers no longer have special
religious status and privilege. . . . The most plausible, straightforward
reading of Galatians 3:26-28 is that it is an acknowledgment of the
fundamental spiritual equality of all categories of people, and a denial
of the relevance of gender, race, or social class to the assignment of
spiritual roles and privileges.[15]

iv) *Galatians 3:28 clearly teaches the spiritual equality of men and
women. Although it is possible to be "equal in status" but have different roles, the traditionalist position does not do this, because it categorically assigns men and women roles of unequal spiritual status.* Thus,
says Groothuis, what one has with different roles is patent *in*equality:

Of course equality can coexist with role differentiation, and of course
"equality does not require sameness," as so many traditionalists

[13] Ibid., 35, italics hers.
[14] Ibid., 27.
[15] Ibid., 35-36.

repeatedly affirm; but these assertions sidestep the challenge that Galatians 3:26-28 presents to the hierarchical gender agenda. Despite traditionalist insistence to the contrary, there *is* a contradiction between the essential, spiritual equality taught in Galatians 3:26-28 and the universal principle of female subordination to male spiritual authority that traditionalists believe is taught elsewhere in the New Testament.[16]

Groothuis points out that the different roles assigned to women are, in reality, *not* equal:

> The idea of spiritual authority as unearned and intrinsic to maleness logically entails the spiritual inferiority of women. In the traditionalist system, the male is considered, solely by virtue of his maleness, to be better suited to represent God to his family and to the church congregation. He is, by implication, more like God and better suited spiritually to access God directly. Such beliefs are incompatible with the clear teaching in Galatians 3:26-28. . . . [17]

So Groothuis affirms that spiritual equality *can* exist along with a differentiation of gender roles, but says that the traditionalist position fails to do this—because it denies equal spiritual opportunity, status, and privilege to women. The spiritual equality taught in Galatians 3:28, says Groothuis, is incompatible with the traditionalist position.[18] "The question that must be addressed is not whether it is *possible* to be equal in being but different in role or rank (for it *is* possible), but whether it is logically and theologically appropriate to describe and defend the traditionalist understanding of women's subordination in these terms."[19]

*v) Texts that appear to define women's and men's roles differently (e.g., 1 Cor. 11, 14; Eph. 5; Col. 3; 1 Tim. 2; 1 Peter 3) are limited in large part by their historical and cultural contexts. These texts ought not*

---

[16] Ibid., 37, italics hers.
[17] Ibid.
[18] Groothuis rightly recognizes that the context of Galatians 3:28 is more theological than social. So, "in order to stay as close as possible to Paul's purpose in writing these words" she builds her case from the spiritual equality taught in Galatians 3:28. It is reasonable, she adds, to expect social implications from this equality, but she intentionally builds her case on the *spiritual* equality taught in Galatians 3:28 (ibid., 27).
[19] Ibid., 42-43, italics hers.

to be regarded as direct statements of a universal principle of male authority but as culturally specific applications of such general moral principles as civil obedience, respect for others, and social property.[20] Groothuis believes that all biblical texts teach norms and principles to which we are bound, and this is true even of texts such as 1 Timothy 2. She believes, however, that some texts state moral and theological principles more directly and are thus more cross-culturally applicable. Galatians 3:28 would fit this category. Groothuis quotes F. F. Bruce's commentary on Galatians: "Paul states the basic principle here [Galatians 3:28]; if restrictions on it are found elsewhere in the Pauline corpus, as in 1 Corinthians 14:34f. . . . or 1 Timothy 2:11f., they are to be understood in relation to Galatians 3:28, and not *vice versa*."[21] The cultural situation of the New Testament church, which was one of social inequality and gender hierarchy, accounts for the New Testament texts that appear to teach male authority in the church and home:

> These texts were written to Christians living in situations of social inequality; yet traditionalists read them as though they were direct statements of a spiritual principle of gender hierarchy literally applicable to modern-day Christians who do *not* live in situations of social inequality. Thus, the New Testament's instructions to the early church, which were intended to show believers how to exercise Christlike mutual submission in the context of an authoritarian, hierarchical society, are taken (or mistaken) to be statements of a universal principle of unilateral female submission to male spiritual authority.[22]

The submission of wives to their husbands (Eph. 5) and women to male leadership in the church (1 Tim. 2) are simply examples of "temporary accommodation[s] to certain functional differences between men and women in ancient patriarchal cultures."[23] Groothuis would fall short of labeling Galatians 3:28 a "normative" text. Given, however, that "the hierarchy texts are limited in part by their historical and cultural contexts,"[24] in her estimation Galatians 3:28 is more directly applicable today.

---

[20] This summary is a rough quotation of Groothuis, ibid., 41-42.
[21] F. F. Bruce, quoted in ibid., 26.
[22] Ibid., 38, italics hers.
[23] Ibid.
[24] Ibid. 41

I trust that these five summary statements fairly and comprehensively present Groothuis's use of Galatians 3:28.

## A RESPONSE[25]

The purpose of this section is not to restate arguments previously put forth but rather to respond specifically to Rebecca Groothuis's use of Galatians 3:28. Pertinent sections of my earlier chapters will be referenced when applicable.

i) Response to Groothuis's assertion that *Galatians 3:28 is the most important verse in the Bible on equality:*

First, Galatians 3:28 itself makes no mention of equality. As we have seen, Paul argues that there is no male/female, Jew/Gentile, slave/free because all are now one in Christ Jesus. He affirms oneness in Christ, *not equality.* While not desiring to dismiss an appropriate sense of equality derived from Galatians 3:28, the absence of any direct mention of equality in that verse should cause us to wonder whether this verse really is the most important verse in the Bible about equality.

Second, this claim is difficult to assess because of the problems associated with calling two things "equal." As we have seen, the nature of two distinct groups of people or things is that they are *both* equal *and* unequal, not simply equal *or* unequal. Groothuis herself admits that equality is a problematic term. What, then, *is* the equality derived from Galatians 3:28, according to Groothuis? She lists several ways that two persons, or groups of persons, can be equal:

> (1) equal human worth, (2) equal ability, (3) equal maturity, (4) equal rights and opportunities, (5) equal status, (6) equal social value, (7) equal identity (being the same, thus interchangeable in any role).[26]

Evangelical egalitarians, according to Groothuis, "affirm all types of equality [1-6] between women and men *except* the equality of identity or sameness [7]."[27] So Groothuis's statement that Galatians 3:28 is the

---

[25] Groothuis's book has far more to say about the issue of manhood and womanhood than her comments on Galatians 3:28. The critique here is not of her entire case for egalitarianism, but simply of her use of Galatians 3:28 in that endeavor.

[26] Groothuis, ibid., 45.

[27] Ibid., 48, italics hers.

most important verse in the Bible on equality means equality as
described in (1–6) but not equality as described in (7).

It is to Groothuis's credit that she delineates different ways in which
two groups of people can be equal. This is certainly more helpful than
a statement such as "Galatians 3:28 teaches that men and women are
equal," as we have already seen that, without a clear standard of comparison and a means of measurement, the term *equal* can be very slip-
pery. Obviously, from her list, Groothuis sees a vast number of ways in
which men and women are "equal," and yet at the same time believes
that men and women are also different (7):

> Obviously, male and female are not identical, nor are male and female
> sexual roles interchangeable. Sexually differentiated roles follow from
> the differences that exist between men and women. However, the sex-
> ually based differences in abilities that do exist between men and
> women—the most notable of which are the different roles in repro-
> duction—do not justify the subordination of one gender to the other.
> Moreover, there are many roles and activities for which these differ-
> ences are largely irrelevant or not determinative.[28]

Yet despite Groothuis's noteworthy efforts to clarify her concept of
equality, one is still left with questions. For example, she writes that men
and women are not interchangeable in just "any" role (7), but when
*spiritual roles* are at stake, she appears to say that men and women *are*
interchangeable:

> The most plausible, straightforward reading of Galatians 3:26-28 is
> that it is an acknowledgment of the fundamental spiritual equality of
> all categories of people, and a *denial of the relevance of gender, race
> or social class to the assignment of spiritual roles* and privileges.[29]

If gender is *irrelevant* to the assignment of spiritual roles, then it
would appear that men and women are interchangeable when it comes
to spiritual roles.

So how does one respond to Groothuis's assertion that Galatians
3:28 is the most important verse in the Bible on equality? To utilize her

---

[28] Ibid.
[29] Ibid., 36, italics mine.

categories, I agree with her that Galatians 3:28 is relevant, at least by implication, to the question of the equality of human worth (1) and possibly equality of opportunity (4), status (5), and social value (6), depending on how one defines these terms. It is not clear to me, however, that Galatians 3:28 addresses equality of abilities (2) or maturity (3). And surely Groothuis and I could partially agree on (7)—that Galatians does *not* teach the interchangeability of men and women. But we differ on whether this verse teaches the irrelevance of gender when it comes to *spiritual* roles in the home and the church.

A final comment is appropriate regarding Groothuis's claim that Galatians 3:28 is the most important verse in the Bible on equality. Such broad, sweeping claims regarding equality and Galatians 3:28 are rhetorically powerful. Galatians 3:28 *does,* after all, have something to say about the equality of men and women. However, when Groothuis claims that "men and women are spiritually equal" in light of Galatians 3:28 and leaves the standard of comparison unspecified or unclear, she would seem to imply that Galatians 3:28 teaches that men and women are equal in a host of other ways as well.

Such a plea for equality is powerful. Who, after all, wants to argue that someone is *un*equal? And who wants to oppose "gender equality"? But to say that Galatians 3:28 is the most important verse in the Bible on equality, leaving "equality" undefined, is confusing at best and deceptive at worst. Consider Westen's comments on Abraham Lincoln's rhetorical use of "equality" in the famous Lincoln-Douglas presidential debates:

> Rhetorically, however, Lincoln used "equality" to his advantage by exploiting two of its persuasive features. He was able to demand equality without having to specify the precise rules by which such equality would be measured. Lincoln's racial views, in fact, were rather complicated. On the one hand, he did not believe that blacks should be granted citizenship or that they should be allowed to vote, sit on juries, hold public office, or intermarry with whites. On the other hand, he did believe that they should be free from the bondage of chattel slavery, at least in the new territories in which slavery had not yet taken hold. By expressing his racial views in the elliptical language of equality, however, he could appeal to people possessing a range of racial views without alerting them to their potential differ-

ences. . . . More importantly, Lincoln exploited the favorable connotations of "equality" and the pejorative connotations of "inequality"
by making himself the champion of equality and Douglas the defender
of inequality.[30]

To be fair, in her book Groothuis has not left "equality" completely
undefined, and I appreciate her efforts to clarify her views. Yet at the
same time I think saying that Galatians 3:28 is the most important verse
in the Bible on equality is dangerously broad and potentially misleading.

So, is Galatians 3:28 the most important verse in the Bible on equality, as Groothuis argues? Yes and no, depending on the standard of comparison. Is it the most important verse describing how all groups of
people, regardless of race, gender, or social status, may equally, without
distinction, become sons of God and inherit the blessings of salvation?
Yes. Is it the most important verse on equal (i.e., interchangeable) roles
of men and women in the home and church? No. It has already been
argued that the lexical data (the possible meanings for "one"), syntax
(the meaning of "you are all one"), and context (the flow of Galatians
3–4 and the structure of 3:26-29) all fail to support the conclusion that
Galatians 3:28 teaches the interchangeability of men's and women's
roles in the family and church. Galatians 3:28 has something to say
about equality, but a close and fair inspection of the biblical text itself
will not allow extraneous notions of equality, foreign to the author's
intention, to be imported into the notion of equality that was actually
intended by the author.

ii) Response to Groothuis's assertion that *Galatians 3:28 describes
one of the theological consequences of the inauguration of the new
covenant, which provides spiritual equality for all, in contrast to the old
covenant, which gave privileged status almost exclusively to freeborn
Jewish males:*
Both sides in the gender debate agree that Galatians 3:28 describes
the people of God in the new covenant. Is it accurate, however, to portray the old covenant as one that gave privileged status almost exclu-

---

[30] Peter Westen, *Speaking of Equality: An Analysis of the Rhetorical Force of 'Equality' in Moral
and Legal Discourse* (Princeton, N.J.: Princeton University Press, 1990), 281-282.

sively to freeborn Jewish males, in contrast to the new, which provides equality to all? Does Galatians, particularly chapters 3–4, present the arrival of Christ and the inauguration of the new covenant in terms of the arrival of new roles, status, and privileges for the "have-nots" of the Old Testament: women, slaves, and Gentiles? Groothuis's attempt to define the old/new contrast as a have-not/have contrast misinterprets Galatians 3:28 and ignores, or at least minimizes, the contrast(s) that Paul himself does make between the new covenant and the old. Several observations are pertinent in this regard.

First, Galatians 3:28 doubtless teaches that all who are in Christ, without distinction, are heirs and sons of God. Each believer has the promised, greatly anticipated Spirit.

Second, though there are changes in the new covenant presented in Galatians 3–4, there is no specific mention of have/have-not class distinctions anywhere in Galatians. Some, such as David Scholer, see Galatians 2:11-14 as providing the perfect example of class distinctions. He states, "I would be tempted to say that Galatians 2:11-14 alone is almost enough evidence to make the whole case for [egalitarianism]."[31] We saw in chapter 1, however, that the *real* issue in 2:11-14 is a salvation-historical problem: How are Jews and Gentiles to relate given the arrival of the new covenant? The *presenting* problem was food regulations; the *underlying* problem was theological. This is clear from the arguments that follow after 2:11-14 and continue throughout most of the book. Paul does not go from 2:11-14 to talk about roles or inequities. He talks about the law, the old covenant, and the arrival of the new. It is reductionistic to view 2:11-14 as illustrative of a have/have-not schema. The Jew/Gentile distinction gets specific attention in Galatians 2 because of its salvation-historical significance, not because it is a nice test case of social inequities. If the focus of the new covenant was rectifying injustices of the old class distinctions, one would expect this to be mentioned, or at least alluded to, somewhere in Galatians.

Third, the contrasts Paul makes in Galatians 3–4 are different than Groothuis's have/have-not paradigm. In the old covenant, for example, God's people were "children . . . in slavery under the basic principles of

---

[31] David M. Scholer, "Galatians 3:28 and the Ministry of Women in the Church," in *Theology, News and Notes* (Pasadena, Calif.: Fuller Theological Seminary, June 1998), 22.

the world," while under the new covenant they "receive the full rights of sons" (4:3, 5). Those Jews who, through faith, were blessed by sharing in the blessings of the promise made to Abraham (3:9) now see the promise come to the Gentiles (3:14). And those who then could only long for the inheritance now can celebrate its arrival (4:7) and subsequent blessings. In summary, Paul does describe (in chapters 3–4) several contrasts between the old and new covenants, but he does not present the new covenant as a time that does away with "special religious status and privilege"[32] for Jews, free people, and men.

Fourth, any have/have-not theme in Galatians 3–4 is not tied to class distinctions such as gender, race, or economic status, but to changes in salvation-history that are relevant to *all* groups of people. Note that it was primarily the *Jews* who were described as slaves awaiting the proper time to become full sons. Freeborn Jewish males were among the "have-nots" in Galatians 3–4! It was *all* Old Testament saints, whether Jew/Gentile, slave/free, male/female, who eagerly awaited the promised inheritance. Galatians does not describe the new covenant as one that brings status and privilege for certain classes of people who were second-class under the old covenant. Paul's emphasis in these chapters is upon the arrival of new blessings for *all* who were held prisoner "until faith should be revealed" (3:23), not upon the arrival of new privileges for particular classes of "un-equal" Old Testament saints.[33]

There are similarities between Groothuis's claim that the new covenant brought privileges to slaves, women, and Gentiles, and the claim previously evaluated, that Galatians 3:28 is about equality. In both cases she has taken a truth that is rightly found in the text and illegitimately added something that is not in the text. She is correct that there is a notion of equality taught in Galatians 3:28, but from this she concludes something foreign to the text—equal (interchangeable) roles. She correctly affirms an old/new contrast in Galatians 3:28, but then defines this contrast in ways foreign to Galatians 3–4 (haves/have-nots based on gender, race, and social class).

---

[32] Groothuis, *Good News*, 35.
[33] This is not to deny that the arrival of the new covenant means unique changes for different groups of people. Jews, for example, experience changes with the arrival of the new covenant, such as the end of ritual sacrifices, that would not be experienced by Gentile believers.

iii) Response to Groothuis's assertion that *Galatians 3:28 means not only that men and women are joint recipients of the blessings of Christ, but also that men and women have equal opportunities to participate in leadership in the home and religious community:*

Here Groothuis again moves from what Galatians 3:28 *does* say— that men and women are joint recipients of the blessings of Christ—to the claim that men and women can have equal opportunities to lead the home and church.

First, even if Galatians 3:28 teaches that men and women are "equal members" in Christ, it does not follow that men and women have "equal opportunities." Both of these "equal statements" need qualification. For, as we have seen, simply because two entities are equal in one respect, it does not follow that they are equal in other respects as well. The twelve tribes were equal "members" of Israel, but each tribe did not have equal (the same) opportunities. Groothuis insists that one implies the other, but this is not the case.

Second, the term "equal opportunity" begs for further clarification. Complementarians think women have "equal opportunity" to serve in the church. "Equal opportunities" can be quite different. For example, perhaps I am offered two very different teaching jobs, one in Seattle and one in Vermont. I can accurately say that they are "equal opportunities" for me, even though the job descriptions might vary widely. So what does Groothuis mean by "equal opportunity"? For Groothuis "equal opportunity to participate in the leadership of the home and church" means "the denial of the relevance of gender . . . to spiritual roles"[34] in the home and church. "Equal opportunity," then, is translated into the affirmation that gender is irrelevant to roles in the home and church. This is another sleight-of-hand regarding the notion of equality. Who can be against "equal opportunity"? By equating "equality" with "interchangeable roles" Groothuis makes a powerful rhetorical claim. But is her claim found in the text of Galatians 3:28 or the context of Galatians 3–4? No.

Galatians 3:28 says nothing specifically about who, if anyone, God has appointed to lead a home or church. Groothuis arrives at this con-

---

[34] Groothuis, *Good News*, 36.

clusion by first insisting that Galatians 3:28 is about spiritual equality, then, building upon this claim to spiritual equality, insisting that this equality means that men and women have equal (interchangeable) roles in the home and church. What does the text say? From the text, "You are all sons of God through faith in Christ Jesus. . . . There is neither Jew nor Greek, slave nor free, male nor female, for you are all one in Christ Jesus. If you belong to Christ, then you are Abraham's seed, and heirs according to the promise" (3:26, 28-29), she concludes that men and women have interchangeable roles in the leadership of the home and church. This conclusion is foreign to Paul's intention. There is nothing in Galatians 3–4, or in the entire book of Galatians, that implies that Paul desired to address the issue of gender roles, even by implication. This silence should cause one at least to be tentative about insisting that Galatians 3:28 is a central verse on the roles of men and women in the home and church.

The leap from "joint blessings in Christ" or "equal spiritual status" to "equal opportunities to participate in leadership in the home and religious community" characterizes virtually all egalitarian teachings on Galatians 3:28. This leap cannot be defended exegetically, as the text simply fails even to hint at the issue of the respective roles of men and women. And the leap is logically inconsistent, for one notion of equality does not imply others.

iv) Response to Groothuis's assertion that *Galatians 3:28 clearly teaches the spiritual equality of men and women. Though it is possible to be "equal in status" but have different roles, the traditionalist position does not do this, because it categorically assigns men and women roles of unequal spiritual status:*
A response to this claim—that complementarians categorically deny women roles of privilege and status—necessarily takes one far from an exegetical study of Galatians 3:28, as it requires that one examine the roles of men and women as found in the New Testament. Given this, only a brief comment is possible.

One of the strengths of Groothuis's book, from an egalitarian perspective, is that she takes on the complementarian claim that it is possible for women to be equal in status while having different roles than men. Groothuis agrees that this is possible, yet is quick to insist that this is *not* the case in the traditionalist/equalitarian struggle, for the different roles given to women are, by her estimation, inferior. Men have "superior positions,"[35] "higher status,"[36] "upper-level positions of social and spiritual authority,"[37] and sit with "privilege"[38] at the head of a "religious pecking order."[39] Groothuis comments, "The normal, commonsensical understanding is that this sort of role differentiation is what distinguishes the privileged (or ruling) class from the underprivileged (or disempowered) class. To construe such a power inequity in any other way is to engage in word games."[40] The bottom line is that complementarians are propagating a caste system—the permanent subordination of one class to another.[41]

It is difficult to find fault with Groothuis's logic. After all, if one class of people permanently subjugates another class of people, assigning to them inferior status and second-class functions, it would be hard to argue that there is any sort of meaningful equality between these classes of people. But is this how complementarians believe the Scriptures present male leadership in the church and home? Do complementarians teach that male/female relationships in the church and home are to be characterized as superior/inferior, privileged/unprivileged, ruling/disempowered, or higher status/lower status? Do the Scriptures *ever* present male/female relationships in these terms, even in those "hierarchy" passages that Groothuis considers to have been written to accommodate a patriarchal culture (Eph. 5; 1 Tim. 2)? Clearly not. Groothuis creates a *false* picture of complementarianism, painting it with categories foreign to Scripture and to complementarianism. Then she judges this male/female paradigm as unfair and worthy of condemnation. Her pronouncement of judgment goes without question, but her false portrayal of the complementarian model of male/female relationships is to be discredited. There is no true correspondence between the model of gender relationships portrayed by Groothuis and the complementarian position or the Bible. Thus, her ardent claim that the traditional position fails to

---

[35] Ibid., 53.
[36] Ibid., 71.
[37] Ibid., 44.
[38] Ibid., 54.
[39] Ibid., 35.
[40] Ibid., 54-55.
[41] Ibid., 51.

be an example of "equal status with different roles" is without merit. She has created a monster that all—egalitarians and complementarians alike—would want to slay.[42]

v) Response to Groothuis's assertion that *texts that appear to define women's and men's roles differently (e.g., 1 Cor. 11, 14; Eph. 5; Col. 3; 1 Tim. 2; 1 Peter 3) are limited in large part by their historical and cultural contexts. These texts ought not to be regarded as direct statements of a universal principle of male authority but as culturally specific applications of such general moral principles as civil obedience, respect for others, and social property:*

This hermeneutical discussion is beyond the bounds of this study. Several articles and books already cited deal with this question.[43] It should be noted, however, that my interpretation of Galatians 3:28 in no way conflicts with Pauline passages that appear to delineate different roles for men and women. Given this interpretation, then, there is no need to declare one text "more directly applicable" and other texts "more culturally bound." When considering what the New Testament says about gender roles, it seems most wise to focus on those texts that

---

[42] There is rhetorical profit in utilizing poignant dichotomies such as superior/inferior, privileged/unprivileged, ruling/disempowered, and higher status/lower status, especially in today's culture. In the end, however, Groothuis critically sabotages her case by criticizing something virtually no one believes. She is culpable of misrepresenting the complementarian position by implying that these dichotomies accurately reflect their beliefs. The following citations are illustrative; many others could be produced: "God's kingdom does not leave room for the totalitarian (absolute and unearned) authority of one person over another, whereby one person 'stands in the place of God' for the other" (ibid., 47). "Could it be that an unprejudiced assessment of biblical teaching finds no compelling evidence of an eternal spiritual principle requiring men to occupy roles of leadership and women to assume roles of subordinate domesticity?" (ibid., 12). "The traditionalist agenda, whereby a man in some sense mediates his wife's relationship with God, is more akin to the old covenant under Mosaic Law than the new covenant described in Galatians 3:26-28" (ibid., 39). "This contrasts sharply with the traditionalist agenda, wherein woman's chief purpose in life is to serve as man's subordinate assistant" (ibid., 60-61). "It stands to reason that anyone who is deemed permanently unfit to occupy the superior position must be inherently incapable of performing that function satisfactorily" (ibid., 53-54). "If women and men enjoy spiritual equality under the new covenant, then this equality is fundamentally contradicted by an exclusively male prerogative to interpret and determine the Word and the will of God authoritatively in the home and in the church" (ibid., 27). These are extreme statements and it would be difficult to find a single complementarian to agree with even one of them. Nothing is to be gained by criticizing a position that virtually nobody espouses.

[43] The articles by Köstenberger and Yarbrough are probably closest to the opinion of this author. Andreas J. Köstenberger, "Gender Passages in the NT: Hermeneutical Fallacies Critiqued," *Westminster Theological Journal* 56 (1994): 259-283; Robert W. Yarbrough, "The Hermeneutics of 1 Timothy 2:9-15," in *Women in the Church: A Fresh Analysis of 1 Timothy 2:9-15*, eds. Andreas Köstenberger, Thomas Schreiner, H. Scott Baldwin (Grand Rapids, Mich.: Baker, 1995), 155-196.

directly address the roles of men and women (e.g., Eph. 5; 1 Tim. 2; Titus 1, 2) rather than trying to settle the issue with Galatians 3:28, a text that makes no statement about or allusion to gender roles.

It is likely that Groothuis's book, and her view on the meaning and significance of Galatians 3:28, will be influential in the coming years. The book is well written, and she has passionately put forward a rhetorically compelling case for the "equality" of men and women. Her message will fall on many receptive ears, for surely women have been mistreated by men in the past and, sadly, this seems likely to continue in the future. All slighted people long deeply, and rightly, to be acknowledged as unique and fully equal reflections of the divine image, and many of these women will find hope in Groothuis's case for gender equality.

Groothuis's use of Galatians 3:28 in this endeavor, however, is critically flawed. She asserts that Galatians 3:28 is the most important verse in the Bible on equality. But this is both imprecise and misleading. Does "for you are all one" directly say anything about equality? If it *implies* something about equality, what *specifically* does it imply? Under the banner of "spiritual equality" Groothuis argues that Galatians 3:28 eliminates the "traditionalist" gender-specific roles in the home and church. This is specious logic; Galatians itself says nothing specifically about gender roles, nor does it imply that any concept of equality that *is* found in Galatians 3:28 precludes "traditionalist" gender roles. Things, or people, are not equal *or* unequal; rather, they are both equal *and* unequal. Simply because Galatians 3:28 contains some notion of equality, it does not follow that the spiritual roles of men and women are interchangeable in the home and church. In many instances Groothuis makes valid conclusions from the text, such as the importance of Galatians 3:28 to the changes in God's people in the new covenant; but then she distorts these truths, such as when she portrays the arrival of the new covenant as a time when all Gentiles, females, and slaves become "equal" with freeborn Jewish males. She validly recognizes some sense of "spiritual equality" in Galatians 3:28; but then, after painting a picture of complementarianism using labels such as superior/inferior, privileged/unprivileged, ruling/disempowered, and higher status/lower status, she concludes that the spiritual equality taught in Galatians 3:28 makes the complementarian position untenable. What is untenable is her portrait of complementarianism. Her argument succeeds against some concocted position, but no complementarian I know will think that Groothuis has put forth a valid argument against his or her position.

# CONCLUSION:
# CLARITY AND CHARITY

This study began with the stated goal of providing *clarity* on the meaning and significance of Galatians 3:28 while dealing *charitably* with those who disagree with my position. As my focused study of this passage comes to a close after more than two years of thought and effort, I still find myself progressing in my knowledge of the text while at the same time striving to be more charitable toward those who disagree with me. I close with some final observations on the need for clarity and charity in the study of Galatians 3:28.

## CLARITY AND GALATIANS 3:28

Galatians 3:28 has emerged as a central text in the contemporary debate over the roles of men and women. Throughout this study our goal has been to understand what Paul meant and did not mean by this verse. Did Paul in Galatians 3:28 teach or imply the interchangeability of the roles of men and women in the home and church? Or did Paul mean something else by this verse? It is important that we strive for *clarity* in our understanding of this text. We cannot settle for confusion.

Clarity will never be possible without focusing on the details of the text. Galatians 3:28, like all Scripture, must be interpreted in its context, allowing the flow of Galatians 3–4, the structure of Galatians 3:26-29, and the meaning of "you are all one" to determine the meaning and significance of this verse. It is *important* to examine the exegetical details of the text. It is amazing how infrequently this is done, especially with Galatians 3:28.

In chapter 4 we looked at Rebecca Groothuis's use of Galatians 3:28 in her book *Good News for Women: A Biblical Picture of Gender Equality.* Although her use of this verse is unique in some respects, much of her argument is representative of how most egalitarians would use this verse. Egalitarians usually start with some sense of "equality" or "spiritual equality" derived from Galatians 3:28 and conclude with the denial of gender-based roles in the home and church. I have shown that this type of argumentation is invalid because it misinterprets Galatians 3:28 and is counter to the nature of "equality." Even if some sense of equality is found in Galatians 3:28, it does not follow that the spiritual roles of men and women in the home and church are interchangeable.

Perhaps an example will best illustrate this tendency to pass over the details of Galatians 3–4 and Galatians 3:28 and focus on other issues. In the introduction I mentioned David Scholer's installation speech as professor of New Testament at Fuller Theological Seminary. He finds four "very compelling reasons" for believing that Galatians 3:28 is *"the fundamental Pauline theological basis for the inclusion of women and men as equal and mutual partners in all the ministries of the church."*[1] These are:

> 1. Galatians 3:28 is clearly a summative expression of an essential part of the central core network of Pauline theology, especially as developed in Galatians.

> 2. It is most likely that the triple pairing found in Galatians 3:28 is an intentional use of a long-standing and culturally diverse tradition and of a somewhat fixed formulaic device. Thus, Paul's theological affirmation in Galatians 3:28 is at the same time a strong statement with traditional and cultural overtones, which identifies the text as horizontal as well as vertical.

> 3. The choice of the three pairings in Galatians 3:28 is not an abstract, capricious, or innocent one. Rather, these three pairings represent three of the most important and critical social and status divisions in Paul's Greco-Roman culture. . . . In order to show the dramatic character, power and reality of the "new creation" established in Christ

---

[1] David M. Scholer, "Galatians 3:28 and the Ministry of Women in the Church," in *Theology, News and Notes* (Pasadena, Calif.: Fuller Theological Seminary, June 1998), 20, italics his.

Jesus, *Paul uses social realities that could not conceivably have been employed in his setting without horizontal implications.*

4. It can be demonstrated that Paul himself actualized in the social-ecclesial realm the horizontal dimensions of the elimination of these three polarities in Christ Jesus. The theological vision of Galatians 3:28 was hermeneutically engaged by Paul in his relationships within the church. This is evidenced, in part, by his letter to Philemon and his active support of twelve women in ministry.[2]

I have addressed two of Scholer's four "compelling reasons" already: In chapter 2 we explored the possibility that Paul was using a fixed formulaic statement such as a baptismal creed (reason 2), and in chapters 2 and 3 we examined Paul's purpose in the choice of the three couplets (reason 3). Reason 4 is beyond the bounds of this study.[3] Of the four reasons Scholer lists for why Galatians 3:28 teaches the "inclusion of women and men as equal and mutual partners in all the ministries of the church," not one directly addresses Paul's argument in Galatians.[4] Granted, these are the words of an installation address and not the contents of a journal article; it is only fair to assume that Scholer has far more to say about Galatians 3:28 than is found in this brief speech. But the four points he does offer are revealing.

What is immediately apparent in Scholer's argument is that his evidences are based more on history, culture, and hermeneutics than on the

---

[2] Ibid., 20-21, italics his.
[3] It is surely a legitimate and necessary task to pull all the biblical evidences on manhood and womanhood together. One of the crucial theses of this work, however, is that Galatians 3:28 has not been fairly interpreted in its context and more attention needs to be given to the exegetical specifics of this text. So this study has specifically *avoided* using 1 Timothy 2 or external evidences such as Paul's partnership with women in ministry to define the meaning of Galatians 3:28; instead it has focused on Galatians 3:28 in the context of Galatians.
[4] Scholer's first argument is that Galatians 3:28 is part of an essential core of Pauline theology. He bases this on the structure of Galatians and other Pauline texts. This is easy to assert, but difficult to confirm, as scholars have proposed numerous different "cores" of Paul's theology. If Scholer means that the Jew/Gentile issue was one of several "cores" of Paul's theology, he would have few critics. But if he means that an essential part of the "core" of Paul's theology includes changes in slave/free and male/female relationships, many would disagree with him. One could fairly say that he has simply asserted what he is trying to prove. In a similar manner Klyne Snodgrass makes an interesting claim about the importance of Galatians 3:28. He writes that Galatians 3:28 is Paul's "basic summary of what it means to be a Christian" (Klyne Snodgrass, "Galatians 3:28: Conundrum or Solution?" *Women, Authority, and the Bible* (Downers Grove, Ill.: InterVarsity, 1986), 173). I respect Dr. Snodgrass, but I do not understand how he can make that statement. Claims that Galatians 3:28 is "at the core of Paul's theology" or that Galatians 3:28 is a "basic summary of what it means to be a Christian" are rhetorically powerful, but they are overstatements.

Galatians text. He cites the Jewish texts of the *Tosephta*, B. C. Sirach, and Josephus. He cites the Greco-Roman sources of Thales, Plato, Diogenes Laertius of Thales, Juvenal, Plutarch, and Lactantius on Plato. He also notes Paul's letter to Philemon, his affirmation of women in ministry in 1 Corinthians 11:2-16, "the explicit pattern of equality and mutuality in 1 Corinthians 7,"[5] and the twelve women Paul mentioned as colleagues in ministry. These are not irrelevant observations, especially to the broader questions of gender roles.

But the reason *Paul* gave for why "there is neither male nor female" is that "you are all one in Christ Jesus." It would be helpful to know how Scholer perceives the relation between these two phrases: How does one get "equality" from a verse that only mentions being "one in Christ"? What is the specific nature of this equality that comes from oneness? What does Scholer think the phrase "there is neither male nor female" means? Are the categories *male* and *female* now *totally* irrelevant in Christ? It would be insightful to know how he believes the three pairs relate; is *everything* that is true of the Jew/Greek pair true of the free/slave and male/female pairs? Or is everything that is true of the male/female pair true of the free/slave pair? It would be nice if Scholer defended his interpretation of Galatians 3:28 using more of the details of the text of Galatians. Perhaps Scholer wasn't able to provide exegetical details from Galatians because this was a speech. After all, if he *had* provided many exegetical details it would have been one unpleasant installation ceremony!

My point is simply that many who view Galatians 3:28 as a critical text in the larger debate over the roles of men and women in the home and church tend to slight the exegetical details of the text. Even allowing Scholer great flexibility given the genre of his presentation, his speech nevertheless is an example of someone explaining the meaning of a text substantially apart from the exegetical details of the text. His "four very compelling reasons" for his interpretation of Galatians 3:28 include a supposed link to a fixed ancient formula, the fact that Greco-Roman and Jewish sources contain anti-women statements, and the fact that Paul worked with Chloe and Junia. I, for one, would be more persuaded by his "very compelling reasons" if he explained the text.

[5] Scholer, "Galatians 3:28," 22. First Corinthians 7 made his speech, but Ephesians 5 didn't.

If we are going to move forward on the meaning and significance of Galatians 3:28, we need to focus on the specifics of the text and the argument as Paul presents it. To move from some notion of equality found in Galatians 3:28 to the denial of gender-based roles in the home and church is invalid because such a conclusion misses Paul's argument as he presents it in Galatians 3–4 and misconstrues the specifics of Galatians 3:28. We need scholars on both sides of this issue to focus more intently on the text if we are to have any hope of clarity.

## CHARITY AND GALATIANS 3:28

It is probably impossible to overstate the emotional nature of the gender debate in the church today. At stake is nothing less than how an individual feels about his or her ministry, self, and role in life. On one hand, in light of Genesis 3:16b we should not be surprised at the existence of tension between men and women. Though complementarians and egalitarians interpret this passage differently, both sides can agree that the Scripture teaches us that men and women will experience substantial strife. Yet on the other hand, one cannot help but marvel at how volatile this debate has become. This is a passionate topic! For this reason, it is even more imperative that we strive to be charitable in our interactions with those with whom we disagree. It is much easier to be cynical, sarcastic, unfair, and spiteful.

In the past few years I have been slowly learning lessons regarding charity. Every week for the past couple of years I have met with a group of people who are quite diverse theologically. These friends are ministers from a wide variety of denominations. In this group I would doubtless be in the minority on many positions, including in this area of the roles of men and women in the home and church. Quite a few of these individuals are dedicated women pastors. This issue is *deeply* important to them. In fact, I remember a statement one colleague made a few months ago: "I dream of the day when my daughter asks me, 'Mom, you mean there was a day when African-Americans were slaves? And a time when women weren't allowed to be pastors? And a time when homosexuals weren't viewed as normal people?'" For this friend, these groups of people share much in common; they are excluded people, kept from full participation in the gospel. At least one of these pastors teaches in the women's studies department at a leading university. Virtually all are committed to some form of religious pluralism/inclusivism that I would find quite objectionable (of course, they would find my position dangerously exclusive). We see the Christian life and God's Word quite differently. Furthermore, we are passionate about our beliefs; they deeply matter to us.

Over the past year we have taken half an hour each week to tell each other our "faith journeys." It would be impossible to do justice to the diversity of those stories! What I've learned through each of the stories is that behind every theological position is a real person, a person with thoughts, needs, and feelings. Hearing my friends' stories has not changed my perspective on Galatians 3:28, but it has taught me a lot about charity. It is indeed inevitable that we will disagree on many issues, including Galatians 3:28, but this doesn't mean that I cannot deal with them with respect and charity. In fact, there is something unique about each of them that is important—they are fellow image-bearers. I can care about them and their lives and families. I can respect them as fellow ministers. I can interact with each of them as I would want them to interact with me. I can represent their positions as they would want them represented. And yet I can wholly disagree with them and hope that they would change their views on Galatians 3:28.

I trust that this work has produced both clarity and charity. It is right that evangelicals go to the Bible to answer questions that have arisen in the struggle over maleness and femaleness, and Galatians 3:28 is certainly one of the texts that must be considered. This discussion should be undertaken with a charitable spirit, one that acknowledges the value of each individual. And yet my goal in this present discussion has been clarity—to determine what Paul intended in Galatians 3:28. I have sought to show that the lexical, syntactical, and contextual evidence points decidedly away from any interpretation that sees in this verse a mandate for interchangeable roles between men and women in the family and church. Such a conclusion, even by way of implication, is not justified by the text.

# APPENDIX

TLG Search for Plural Forms of Ἐιμί Within 6 Words of Εἷς Μιά, or Ἐν Second Century B.C.—First Century A.D.

| Plural Forms of Ἐιμί | Εἷς | Μιά | Ἐν |
|---|---|---|---|
| Present Indicatives | | | |
| ἐσμέν | 2 | 0 | 4 |
| | — | — | (4) |
| ἐστέ | 2 | 1 | 2 |
| | (2) | — | — |
| εἰσίν | 12 | 11 | 11 |
| | (1) | (2) | (2) |
| εἰσί | 4 | 6 | 2 |
| | (1) | — | — |
| Future Indicatives | | | |
| ἐσόμεθα | 0 | 0 | 0 |
| ἔσεσθε | 0 | 0 | 0 |
| ἔσονται | 2 | 2 | 1 |
| | — | — | — |
| Imperfect Indicatives | | | |
| ἦμεν | 0 | 0 | 1 |
| | — | — | — |
| ἦμεθα | 0 | 0 | 0 |
| ἦτε | 0 | 1 | 0 |
| | — | — | — |
| ἦσαν | 3 | 8 | 3 |
| | — | — | — |
| Subjunctives | | | |
| ὦμεν | 0 | 0 | 0 |
| ἦτε | 0 | 1 | 0 |
| | — | — | — |
| ὦσιν | 0 | 2 | 7 |
| | — | — | (5) |
| ὦσι | 0 | 0 | 0 |

*Note:* The figures in the table without parentheses are the number of hits that resulted from each TLG search. The figures within the parentheses are the number of hits that were determined to be parallels to Galatians 3:28 (where a plurality of people or things were said to be "one"). Many of the hits did not fit this paradigm for a variety of reasons and were, as a result, no help for ascertaining the meaning of Galatians 3:28. For example, many hits had the plural form of εἰμί in one clause but the form of "one" occurred in a completely different clause. Only nominative forms of εἷς, μιά, and ἕν were pursued in light of their use with a copulative verb.

This table documents sixteen parallels to Galatians 3:28. The specific passages can be found on pages 73-75.

# BIBLIOGRAPHY

Ayers, David J. "The Inevitability of Failure: The Assumptions and Implementations of Modern Feminism." In *Recovering Biblical Manhood and Womanhood,* eds. John Piper and Wayne Grudem, 312-331. Wheaton, Ill.: Crossway, 1991.

Barclay, John M. G. "Mirror-Reading a Polemical Letter: Galatians as a Test Case." *Journal for the Study of the New Testament* 31 (1987): 73-93.

Barrett, C. K. *From First Adam to Last: A Study in Pauline Theology.* New York: Charles Scribner's Sons, 1962.

———. *Freedom and Obligation: A Study of the Epistle to the Galatians.* Philadelphia: Westminster, 1985.

Bartling, Walter. "The New Creation in Christ." *Concordia Theological Monthly* 21 no. 6 (June 1950): 401-418.

Beasley-Murray, G. R. *Baptism in the New Testament.* Grand Rapids, Mich.: Eerdmans, 1962.

———. "Baptism." In *Dictionary of Paul and His Letters,* ed. Gerald F. Hawthorne and Ralph P. Martin, 60-66. Downers Grove, Ill.: InterVarsity, 1993.

Beker, J. C. *Paul the Apostle: The Triumph of God in Life and Thought.* Philadelphia: Fortress, 1980.

Betz, H. D. *A Commentary on Paul's Epistle to the Galatians.* Hermeneia. Philadelphia: Fortress, 1979.

Bilezikian, Gilbert. *Beyond Sex Roles.* Grand Rapids, Mich.: Baker, 1985.

———. "Hermeneutical Bungee-Jumping: Subordination in the Godhead." *Journal of the Evangelical Theological Society* 40 (1997): 57-68.

Bonneau, Normand. "The Curse of the Law in Gal. 3:10-14." *Novum Testamentum* 39, no. 1 (1997): 60-80.

Boomsma, Clarence. *Male and Female, One in Christ: New Testament Teaching on Women in Office.* Grand Rapids, Mich.: Baker, 1993.

Boucher, Madeleine. "Some Unexplored Parallels to 1 Cor 11,11-12 and Gal 3,28: The NT on the Role of Women." *Catholic Biblical Quarterly* 31 (1969): 50-58.

Boyd, Ian T. E. "Galatians 3:28c: Male and Female Related in Christ." M.A. thesis, Covenant Theological Seminary, 1994.

Brown, Harold O. J. "The New Testament Against Itself: 1 Timothy 2:9-15 and the 'Breakthrough' of Galatians 3:28." In *Women in the Church: A Fresh Analysis of 1 Timothy 2:9-15,* eds. Andreas J. Köstenberger, Thomas R. Schreiner, and H. Scott Baldwin, 197-208. Grand Rapids, Mich.: Baker, 1995.

Bruce, F. F. *The Epistle to the Galatians.* New International Greek Testament Commentary. Grand Rapids, Mich.: Eerdmans, 1982.

Burton, E. de Witt. *A Critical and Exegetical Commentary on the Epistle to the Galatians.* International Critical Commentary. Edinburgh: T. & T. Clark, 1921.

Caneday, A. B. "The Curse of the Law and the Cross: Works of the Law and Faith in Galatians 3:1-14." Ph.D. dissertation, Trinity Evangelical Divinity School, 1992.

Carson, Donald A. "Pauline Inconsistency: Reflections on 1 Corinthians 9:19-23 and Galatians 2:11-14." *Churchman* 100 (1986): 6-45.

————. *The Gospel According to John.* Grand Rapids, Mich.: Eerdmans, 1991.

————. *The Gagging of God: Christianity Confronts Pluralism.* Grand Rapids, Mich.: Zondervan, 1996.

Cline, George J. "The Middle Voice in the New Testament." Th.M. thesis, Grace Theological Seminary, 1983.

Coble, Ann. "The Lexical Horizon of 'One in Christ': The Use of Galatians 3:28 in the Progressive-Historical Debate over Women's Ordination." Th.M. thesis, Covenant Theological Seminary, 1995.

Cousar, Charles B. *A Theology of the Cross: The Death of Jesus in the Pauline Letters.* Minneapolis: Fortress, 1990.

Cranfield, C. E. B. "St. Paul and the Law." *Scottish Journal of Theology* 17 (1964): 43-68.

————. "Changes of Person and Number in Paul's Epistles." In *Paul and Paulinism: Essays in Honour of C. K. Barrett,* ed. M. D. Hooker and S. G. Wilson, 280-89. London: SPCK, 1982.

Crouch, James E. *The Origin and Intention of the Colossian Haustafel.* Göttingen, Germany: Vandenhoeck & Ruprecht, 1972.

Cullman, Oscar. *Salvation in History.* Trans. Sidney Sowers and others. New York: Harper & Row, 1965.

Davies, W. D. *Paul and Rabbinic Judaism.* London: SPCK, 1962.

Davis, John J. "Some Reflections on Galatians 3:28, Sexual Roles, and Biblical Hermeneutics." *Journal of the Evangelical Theological Society* 19 (1976): 201-208.

Donaldson, T. L. "The 'Curse of the Law' and the Inclusion of the Gentiles: Galatians 3:13-14." *New Testament Studies* 32 (1986): 94-112.

Dunn, James D. G. *Baptism in the Holy Spirit.* London: SCM Press, 1977.

————. *Jesus, Paul, and the Law: Studies in Mark and Galatians.* Louisville, Ky.: Westminster/John Knox, 1990.

————. *The Epistle to the Galatians.* Black's New Testament Commentaries. Peabody, Mass.: Hendrickson, 1993.

————. *The Epistles to the Colossians and to Philemon: A Commentary on the Greek Text.* New International Greek Testament Commentary Series. Grand Rapids, Mich.: Eerdmans, 1996.

Ferguson, Sinclair B. "The Reformed Doctrine of Sonship." In *Pulpit and People: Essays in Honour of William Still on His 75th Birthday,* eds. Nigel M. de. S. Cameron and Sinclair Ferguson, 81-88. Edinburgh: Rutherford House, 1986.

Fitzmeyer, Joseph. *Romans: A New Translation with Introduction and Commentary.* The Anchor Bible Series. New York: Doubleday, 1993.

Fuller, Daniel P. "Paul and the Works of the Law." *Westminster Theological Journal* 38 (1975): 28-42.

————. "Paul and Galatians 3:28." *Theological Students Bulletin* 9, no. 2 (1985): 8-13.

Fung, Ronald Y. K. "Ministry in the New Testament." In *The Church in the Bible and the World*, ed. D. A. Carson, 154-212. Grand Rapids, Mich.: Baker, 1987.

———. *The Epistle to the Galatians*. The New International Commentary on the New Testament. Grand Rapids, Mich.: Eerdmans, 1988.

Gasque, W. Ward. "Response." In *Women, Authority, and the Bible*, ed. Alvera Mickelsen, 188-192. Downers Grove, Ill.: InterVarsity, 1986.

Glasswell, M. E. "Some Issues of Church and Society in Light of Paul's Eschatology." In *Paul and Paulinism: Essays in Honour of C. K. Barrett*, eds. M. D. Hooker and S. G. Wilson, 310-319. London: SPCK, 1982.

Gordon, T. David. "The Problem at Galatia." *Interpretation* 41 (1987): 32-43.

Grenz, Stanley J. "Anticipating God's New Community: Theological Foundations for Women in Ministry." *Journal for the Evangelical Theological Society* 38 (1995): 595-611.

Grenz, Stanley J. with Denise Muir Kjesbo. *Women in the Church: A Biblical Theology of Women in Ministry*. Downers Grove, Ill: InterVarsity, 1995.

Groothuis, Rebecca Merrill. *Good News for Women: A Biblical Picture of Gender Equality*. Grand Rapids, Mich.: Baker, 1997.

Grudem, Wayne. "Asbury Professor Advocates Egalitariansim But Undermines Biblical Authority." In *CBMW News*, vol. 2, no. 1 (December 1996), 8-12.

Gundry, Patricia. "Why We're Here." In *Women, Authority, and the Bible*, ed. Alvera Mickelsen, 10-21. Downers Grove, Ill.: InterVarsity, 1986.

Günther, W. and J. Krienke. "Remnant." In *The New International Dictionary of New Testament Theology*, ed. Colin Brown, 247-254. Grand Rapids, Mich.: Zondervan, 1971.

Hansen, G. Walter. *Abraham in Galatians: Epistolary and Rhetorical Contexts*. Journal for the Study of the New Testament Supplement Series 29. Sheffield: JSOT, 1989.

Harris, Murray J. "Prepositions and Theology in the Greek New Testament." In *The New International Dictionary of New Testament Theology*, 3 vols., ed. Colin Brown, 3:1171-1215. Grand Rapids, Mich.: Zondervan, 1971.

Hester, James D. *Paul's Concept of Inheritance: A Contribution to the Understanding of Heilsgeschichte*. Scottish Journal of Theology Occasional Papers, no. 14. Edinburgh: Oliver and Boyd, 1968.

Hong, In-Gyu. *The Law in Galatians*. Journal for the Study of the New Testament Supplement Series 81. Sheffield: JSOT, 1993.

Hurley, James B. *Man and Woman in Biblical Perspective*. Grand Rapids, Mich.: Zondervan, 1981.

Jewett, Paul K. *Man as Male and Female*. Grand Rapids, Mich.: Eerdmans, 1975.

Johnson, S. Lewis. "Role Distinctions in the Church: Gal 3:28." In *Recovering Biblical Manhood and Womanhood*, eds. John Piper and Wayne Grudem, 154-164. Wheaton, Ill.: Crossway, 1991.

Keener, Craig. *Paul, Women, and Wives*. Peabody, Mass.: Hendrickson, 1992.

King, Martin Luther, Jr. "I Have a Dream." Speech given in Washington D.C., August 28, 1963. In *A Testament of Hope: The Essential Writings of Martin Luther*

*King, Jr.*, ed. James Melvin Washington, 219-220. San Francisco: Harper & Row, 1986.

Knight, George W., III. *The Role Relationship of Men and Women: New Testament Teaching.* Chicago: Moody, 1985.

Köstenberger, Andreas. "Gender Passages in the NT: Hermeneutical Fallacies Critiqued." *Westminster Theological Journal* 56 (1994): 259-283.

Kovach, Stephen D. "Egalitarians Revamp Doctrine of the Trinity: Bilezikian, Grenz and the Kroegers Deny Eternal Subordination of the Son." *CBMW News*, vol. 2, no. 1 (December 1996): 1-5.

Kruse, Colin G. "Human Relationships in the Pauline Corpus." In *The Fullness of Time: Biblical Studies in Honour of Archbishop Donald Robinson*, eds. David Petersen and John Pryor, 167-184. Homebush West, NSW: Lancer, 1992.

———. *Paul, the Law, and Justification.* Leicester, England: Apollos, 1996.

Lightfoot, J. B. *Saint Paul's Epistle to the Galatians: A Revised Text, with Introduction, Notes, and Dissertations.* Andover: W. F. Draper, 1870.

Loewe, Raphael. *The Position of Women in Judaism.* London: SPCK, 1966.

Longenecker, Richard N. *New Testament Social Ethics for Today.* Grand Rapids, Mich.: Eerdmans, 1984.

———. *Galatians.* Word Biblical Commentary. Dallas: Word, 1990.

Luther, Martin. *A Commentary on St. Paul's Epistle to the Galatians.* Westwood, N.J.: Fleming H. Revell, 1953.

Lyall, Francis. *Slaves, Citizens, and Sons: Legal Metaphors in the Epistles.* Grand Rapids, Mich.: Zondervan, 1984.

Meyer, Heinrich. *Epistle to the Galatians.* Trans. G. H. Venables. New York: Funk & Wagnalls, 1884.

Montefiore, C. G. and H. Loewe. *A Rabbinic Anthology.* Cleveland, Ohio: World, 1963.

Moo, Douglas J. "'Law,' 'Works of the Law' and Legalism in Paul." *Westminster Theological Journal* 45 (1983): 73-100.

———. "Paul and the Law in the Last Ten Years." *Scottish Journal of Theology* 40 (1987): 287-307.

Neuer, Werner. *Man and Woman in Christian Perspective.* Trans. Gordon J. Wenham. Wheaton, Ill: Crossway, 1991.

O'Brien, Peter T. *Colossians, Philemon.* Word Biblical Commentary. Waco, Tex.: Word, 1982.

———. "Divine Analysis and Comprehensive Solution: Some Priorities from Ephesians 2." *The Reformed Theological Review* 53:3 (September–December 1994): 130-142.

Oerke, A. "ἀνήρ." *TDNT*, 1: 360-363.

Olasky, Susan. "The Feminist Seduction of the Evangelical Church: Femme Fatale." *World*, March 29, 1997, 14.

Osborne, Grant R. "Hermeneutics and Women in the Church." *Journal of the Evangelical Theological Society* 20 (1977): 337-352.

————. *The Hermeneutical Spiral: A Comprehensive Introduction to Biblical Interpretation*. Downers Grove, Ill.: InterVarsity, 1991.

Philo. *The Works of Philo*. Updated edition. Trans. C. D. Yonge. Peabody, Mass.: Hendrickson, 1993.

Piper, John and Wayne Grudem. "An Overview of Central Concerns: Questions and Answers." In *Recovering Biblical Manhood and Womanhood*, eds. John Piper and Wayne Grudem, 60-92. Wheaton, Ill.: Crossway, 1992.

Ridderbos, H. N. *Paul: An Outline of His Theology*. Trans. J. Richard de Witt. Grand Rapids, Mich.: Eerdmans, 1975.

Robinson, D. W. B. "The Distinction Between Jewish and Gentile Believers in Galatians." *Australian Biblical Review* 13 (1965): 29-48.

Sand, A. "ἐπαγγελία." *EDNT*, 2:13-16.

Sanders, E. P. *Paul, the Law, and the Jewish People*. Philadelphia: Fortress, 1983.

Scholer, David. "Galatians 3:28 and the Ministry of Women in the Church." In *Theology, News, and Notes*, 19-22. Pasadena, Calif.: Fuller Theological Seminary, June 1998.

Schreiner, T. R. *The Law and Its Fulfillment: A Pauline Theology of the Law*. Grand Rapids, Mich.: Baker, 1993.

Scott, James M. *Adoption as Sons of God: An Exegetical Investigation into the Background of HUIOTHESIA in the Pauline Corpus*. Wissenschaftliche Untersuchungen zum Neuen Testament 2.48. Tübingen: J. C. B. Mohr, 1992.

Seifrid, Mark A. *Justification by Faith: The Origin and Development of a Central Pauline Theme*. Leiden, Netherlands: E. J. Brill, 1992.

————. "In Christ." In *The Dictionary of Paul and His Letters*, eds. Gerald F. Hawthorne and Ralph P. Martin, 433-436. Downers Grove, Ill.: InterVarsity, 1993.

Setiawan, Kornelius A. "An Exegetical Study of Gal. 3:23-29 with Special Reference to Gal. 3:28." Th.M. thesis, Calvin Theological Seminary, 1991.

Snodgrass, Klyne. "Galatians 3:28—Conundrum or Solution?" In *Women, Authority, and the Bible*, ed. Alvera Mickelsen, 161-181. Downers Grove, Ill.: InterVarsity, 1986.

Spicq, Ceslas. *Theological Lexicon of the New Testament*. Trans. and ed. James D. Ernest. Peabody, Mass.: Hendrickson, 1994.

Stählin, G. "ἴσος." *TDNT*, 3:343-355.

Stanley, Susie C. "Response." In *Women, Authority, and the Bible*, ed. Alvera Mickelsen, 181-188. Downers Grove, Ill.: InterVarsity, 1986.

Stauffer, E. "εἶς." *TDNT*, 2:434-442.

Stendahl, Krister. *The Bible and the Role of Women: A Case Study in Hermeneutics*. Trans. Emilie T. Sander. Philadelphia: Fortress, 1966.

*Tanna debe Eliyyahu*. Trans. William G. Braude and Israel J. Kapstein. Philadelphia: Jewish Publication Society of America, 1981.

Thompson, David L. "Women, Men, Slaves and the Bible: Hermeneutical Inquiries." *Christian Scholar's Review* 25 (1996): 326-349.

VanGemeren, Willem A. "Abba in the Old Testament?" *Journal of the Evangelical Theological Society* 31 (1988): 385-398.

Wanke, J. " Ἕλλην." *EDNT*, 1:435-436.

Westen, Peter. *Speaking of Equality: An Analysis of the Rhetorical Force of "Equality" in Moral and Legal Discourse.* Princeton, N.J.: Princeton University Press, 1990.

Westerholm, Stephen. *Israel's Law and the Church's Faith: Paul and His Recent Interpreters.* Grand Rapids, Mich.: Eerdmans, 1988.

Williams, Sam. "Justification of the Spirit in Galatians." *Journal for the Study of the New Testament* 29 (1987): 91-100.

————. "*Promise* in Galatians: A Reading of Paul's Reading of Scripture." *Journal of Biblical Literature* 107 (1988): 709-720.

Windisch, H. "Ἕλλην." *TDNT*, 2:504-516.

Witherington, Ben. "Rite and Rights for Women—Galatians 3:28." *New Testament Studies* 27 (1981): 593-604.

Wright, N. T. *The Climax of the Covenant.* Minneapolis: Fortress, 1991.

Yarbrough, Robert W. "The Hermeneutics of 1 Timothy 2:9-15." In *Women in the Church: A Fresh Analysis of 1 Timothy 2:9-15*, eds. Andreas J. Köstenberger, Thomas R. Schreiner, and H. Scott Baldwin, 155-196. Grand Rapids, Mich.: Baker, 1995.

————. "Heilsgeschichte." In *Evangelical Dictionary of Theology*, 2d ed., ed. Walter Elwell. Grand Rapids, Mich.: Baker, forthcoming.

# GENERAL INDEX

# SCRIPTURE INDEX